M. de Angeli
1972

FIDDLESTRINGS

Other books by Marguerite de Angeli

TED AND NINA GO TO THE GROCERY STORE

TED AND NINA SPEND A HAPPY RAINY DAY

HENNER'S LYDIA

PETITE SUZANNE

COPPER-TOED BOOTS

SKIPPACK SCHOOL

A SUMMER DAY WITH TED AND NINA

THEE HANNAH!

ELIN'S AMERIKA

UP THE HILL

YONIE WONDERNOSE

TURKEY FOR CHRISTMAS

BRIGHT APRIL

JARED'S ISLAND

THE DOOR IN THE WALL

JUST LIKE DAVID

BOOK OF NURSERY AND MOTHER GOOSE RHYMES

BLACK FOX OF LORNE

THE OLD TESTAMENT

A POCKET FULL OF POSIES

MARGUERITE DE ANGELI'S BOOK OF FAVORITE HYMNS

THE GOOSE GIRL

BUTTER AT THE OLD PRICE

FIDDLESTRINGS

by Marguerite de Angeli

DOUBLEDAY & COMPANY, INC.

GARDEN CITY, NEW YORK

1974

ISBN: 0-385-08218-5 Trade
0-385-08437-4 Prebound
Library of Congress Catalog Card Number 73-82243
Copyright © 1974 by Marguerite de Angeli
All Rights Reserved
Printed in the United States of America
First Edition

For my husband
Dai
and for our children
who remembered all these tales,
and for our grandchildren
and great-grandchildren
with my love

ME deA

FIDDLESTRINGS

CHAPTER 1

"It's SPRING!" Dai yelled as he ran out the door, sniffing the warm freshness, and seeing tiny beginnings of leaves on the poplars. Well, almost spring—time for tops and shinny and baseball.

Baseball! How I love it! he thought. There was Butch running to join Ted, who was already thump-thumping the ball into his mitt. Frank came yelling around the corner and as if by some magic signal there they all were ready to begin.

They were playing in the street near Shafer's.

Dai was pitcher and Ted catcher. Butch was at bat. The game went on for a few minutes with no score. Then Dai looked at Ted for a signal and heard him clear his throat and say to Butch, "Butch, your shoelace is untied!"

As Butch looked at his shoe, Dai threw the ball. Butch swung at it, but missed. "STRIKE ONE!" Dai yelled. He was umpire at the moment as well as pitcher.

At that instant, he heard his mother calling—"Dailey-e-e-e!" He knew what that meant, *practice*. Instead of answering, he pitched the ball again.

"Dailey! Come in at once. You know it is lesson day."

"Oh, awright!" He threw down the glove and ball. It wasn't his glove anyway.

Butch laughed and made a face. "Go on, go on! Your ma's calling."

Ted was disgusted. "You always have to practice," he said, "and we just got started. How can we play without a pitcher? We never get to finish a game!" He threw his glove down too. Dai went slowly down the street and up the steps where Roy rushed out to greet him, prancing on his three legs.

"Cheer up!" Mama said. "Your face is as long as your fiddle. Come, wash and change your clothes while I get your lunch. Then you can practice awhile before you go."

"If only I didn't have to go through those endless scales on that baby-sized fiddle, I wouldn't mind so much."

"I know." Mama looked at him. "But it's just that monotonous work that trains your hands so they will almost think for you. It's hard to come in when the boys want you to play ball. I expect Papa to come home tonight and he will be pleased if you are doing well and he *won't* be pleased if you are *not.*"

Mama held Roy's leash and took him with her into the kitchen where Grandma Craig was setting the table.

Dai clumped into the parlor, sticking his tongue out at the portrait of Great-grandfather Benedict, who had started all this fiddle business. Just because he had played the violin because he liked it, why do I have to leave the ball game, Dai thought angrily? As he opened the lid of the fiddle case he remembered that day long ago when Mama was cleaning the parlor. Everything was out of place and Papa noticed the shabby old violin case that always stood back in a corner.

"You know," he said, "I always wanted to play that violin, but, somehow, there never was time. I went to work as a boy and when work was done, I was too tired. That old fiddle was brought to this country when my grandfather Benedict came here with his family from Corsica. It was made in Italy by one of the good violin makers." He took the fiddle out of its case and showed Mama and Dai its delicate carving and firm construction. "It has a certain value," he said, "and when you are old enough it will be yours. I hope you will learn to play it well enough to be a professional." He put the violin back and closed the case.

And so at six Dai had begun to take violin lessons, first with a small instrument. That, he thought ruefully, was when all the practicing began. At nine the small violin had been changed for the next size. Now, at eleven, he was outgrowing that. His eleventh birthday had come and gone while Papa was away on tour. Dai had hoped for a present from him or at least a card. But no present came and no word. Mama had a cake with candles. She made him a new shirt and gave him a new black silk tie. Grandma Craig gave him a brass inkwell in the shape of an armadillo that her father had made of brass, but polished till it looked like gold. Dai had never seen it before because it had been hidden in Grandma's trunk. It had been a very happy birthday but it seemed as if Papa had forgotten him. But then he laughed to himself as he remembered Papa's jokes, the trick he had of putting a warm coffee spoon on Dai's hand to surprise him and make him laugh, the way he sat tickling Dai's neck while he told why he had changed his stage name to Murphy. And after all, none of the other boys in school had an actor for a father.

Papa was a member of the Carncross Minstrels in Philadelphia. At certain seasons, the troupe went on tour and once, when the show was in Chicago, Papa happened to be near the box office when two men stopped to look at the pictures of the partners, Turner and de Angeli. "Turner and de Angeli," one of them said. "I'll bet his name is Murphy."

"Aha!" Papa said, as he told Dai the story one day, "I thought, what a good idea. I'll *be* Murphy. And right then, I began to use the name in the theater. After that, it was John Turner and John E. Murphy. Sometimes, the neighbors called Mama 'Mrs. Murphy,' but she didn't mind, and she doesn't now, do you, Kate?"

"Of course not. I'm proud to be your Mrs. Murphy." Mama laughed.

"I wish I could be an actor instead of a violin player and travel all over as you do," said Dai.

But Papa said, "No no, it is a very uncertain way of making a living. Stick to your fiddle. Some day, you will be a professional and play at the Academy of Music."

Dai watched the clock on the mantel shelf as he went over and over the scales. Promptly, at the end of the half-hour, he put them aside and opened the book to the pieces he was practicing for the school concert—Raff's "Cavatina," and "Traumerei," in case they should want an encore.

Mr. Bucholz had reminded him to be especially careful of the turn of notes in the third phrase. It must be evenly played to give the effect intended by the composer. Dai really loved to play the piece, but would rather die than admit it to anyone, especially the boys on the team. They knew he played the violin. They had heard him at school concerts and though they still teased him, they no longer called him "Sissie!" He was too good at baseball, swimming, and in a fight for that. The fiddle was simply not mentioned.

While Dai practiced, Roy lay outside the parlor door. He whined when a minor chord hurt his ears but seemed to know that he must be quiet or Mama would put him out.

Dai glanced at the clock. Fifteen minutes to go. Time to play the piece for the school concert once more. He drew the bow over the strings with delight in the tone of the low notes and the more even quality he was now able to bring out by the strengthening of his fingers. He was quite lost in the music when Mama called.

Dai laid the fiddle on the piano, but as he did so, remembered the voice of his teacher with its

German accent, saying, "A violin iss as sensitive as a person. Keep it warm and dry, but not too dry. Chusst right. Too much heat warps the delicate wood. Dampness draws the strings and breaks them. Take good care of your instrument and it will serve you long."

Dai put the violin in its place in the case, the bow in the hinged clips in the lid, laid the velvet cover Mama had made over the fiddle, thinking how much he wished for a full-sized one. When would he be old enough to have Great-grandfather's fiddle? He glanced up at Benedict's portrait hanging on the wall.

Roy leaped up joyfully as Dai opened the parlor door, going three-skip-one after him to the kitchen. Roy was three-legged because last winter, chasing a trolley car, biting at the wheels, he had gone too close and had lost his hind leg. Dai had taken him to the University Clinic every day until the wound was healed. Roy was as eager as ever to chase sticks or do anything Dai asked of him, but he tired more easily than before.

Mama, as always, when she was happily busy, was half humming, half whistling a tuneless theme. It had no real melody but was a part of her as were her funny remarks. Mama was a tiny woman with the wiry strength many small people have. Yet Dai knew that she often felt faint when something startled or frightened her. Perhaps, he thought, she had never quite recovered from the tragic drowning of his brother Dan when he was six. But in spite of that she was witty and quick with an an-

swer. If she and Grandma Craig were talking and Dai happened to say "Who?" or "What?" she would answer "Rocky Dumps" or "Mrs. Crib-Pusher." It was always said with a wink so it didn't hurt, yet, was a reminder that what grownups talked about was no concern of Dai's.

As Dai took his fiddle case, ready to leave for his lesson, Mama straightened the collar of his jacket and gave a twist to his tie. She held Roy's collar so he wouldn't follow Dai to the trolley. "Don't forget to bring your fiddle and music home before you stop for your papers!" she called after him. "I won't!" he called back.

All the way to Mr. Bucholz's studio on Spruce Street he whistled the melody of the cavatina. Could he remember the turn and how to play the pianissimo softly?

After he had played the usual studies, Dai played the cavatina as well as he knew how. At the end Mr. Bucholz patted his shoulder and said, "Goot! Goot! You have improved. But I see you will soon need a larger fiddle. The arms are getting too long for that one.

"Now, let us move on to something else." He shuffled through a pile of music to find something suitable, then picked up his own violin and played one of Joachim's compositions. The deep, rich tone vibrated through Dai's whole being. Could he ever play like that?

When Dai thanked him, Mr. Bucholz said, "Yes, it iss fine music. Of what use iss it to play, Dailey, unless what you play iss goot music, yes? If you learn to play what iss goot from the start, you will never be satisfied with less-not."

That afternoon, when Dai was delivering his papers, whistling as usual, he dropped Mrs. Farrell's on her porch just as she opened the door.

She growled at him. "Stop that infernal whistling! Can't you ever be quiet?" She slammed the door. Dai went on his way, sobered, but puzzled, too.

Why was Mrs. Farrell so cross? Anyway, he thought, she's got a face like a sucked orange.

It was suppertime when Dai finished his paper route and he knew as soon as he entered the house that Papa was home. There was that certain fragrance of shaving cream or something, and he flew to the kitchen where Mama was getting supper. Grandma Craig was putting the last things on the table in the dining room and there was Papa with his rosy cheeks, his blue eyes, and open arms.

As they sat down, Papa said, "Well, son, I hear you are doing pretty well with that fiddle of yours. Keep at it. Some day you may be famous. For now, just do every day's practice as well as you can. Your music will be a source of joy all your life, whatever happens."

While they were eating, Dai remembered Mrs. Farrell's scolding.

"Say, what's the matter with that old lady down the street? She bawled me out for whistling. What's the matter with *whis*tling?"

"Nothing," Mama said soothingly, "nothing. Don't mind her; just stop whistling when you come near her house. She's old and she's never had any boys, poor woman. She doesn't know that boys and whistling go together. Just forgive her. Probably it's herself she doesn't like." And Dai thought, but didn't say, "She looks as if she had just bitten into a quince."

"Be nice to her," Mama said. "Remember, she is all alone."

"I'll try," Dai said. It wouldn't be much fun to be all alone.

When they finished supper, Papa said, "I think it's about time for that present I have for you, Dailey. I couldn't very well send it and I meant to write you, but at the time of your birthday, we were moving so fast from one place to another, I had no time. Come." He took Dai's arm and they all went into the parlor. Mama had a secret smile.

Hidden behind a chair was a brand-new fiddle case, and inside the beautiful old violin that had belonged to Great-grandfather Benedict de Angeli.

Dai's jaw dropped.

"Oh-o-o, is it really *mine* now? Oh-o-o!"

Papa lifted it out of the velvet-lined case and held it to the light where Dai could see the exquisite workmanship and rich color. Dai took it in his hands, feeling the satin-smooth neck of the fiddle, turning it to see the matched grain of the back.

"I can't believe it!" he said, tucking it under his chin. "I can't believe it! Now I won't have to bend double when I play. It's great! Thanks!" He tuned the strings and drew the bow over them. "It's got a great sound! Listen!" He opened the music case, took out the cavatina, and played it. There were some blurred notes and some mistakes, the bow being heavier and somewhat longer and the intervals spaced differently from the smaller fiddle, but Dai managed quite well.

"It will take me a little while to get used to it. But now I will be more interested in playing. Now, I'll really practice." He looked up at Great-grandfather Benedict's portrait and felt a little guilty.

CHAPTER 2

The next Saturday, when Dai went for his lesson, Mr. Bucholz was pleased to see Dai's new-old fiddle. He examined it thoroughly, nodding his head and making little sounds of approval. "U-hum, um-hum, it iss in the old tradition, beautiful craftsmanship. Now, my boy, let us see how you can handle it. It will be a little strange at first, but your hands are growing." He sat down at the piano and signaled for Dai to begin.

The past week's practice had accustomed Dai to the larger size of the violin, but it was still more of an effort to balance the bow and to press the strings on the exact notes.

"Give it time," Mr. Bucholz said. "It will come to you."

About two weeks later, as Dai was coming up the street after his lesson, the boys were in the midst of a game right in front of the house. The impulse to join them was so strong that Dai dropped his music and the fiddle case on the mounting block in front of the house and reached for a ball that Chad had aimed at Ted.

Ted ran to catch it, collided with Dai, and

crashed down on top of the fiddle case, breaking it and jamming the lid. Dai was horrified. Was his new fiddle broken? Great-grandfather's fiddle? He tried to pry the lid open as Ted and the boys gathered round him, but it stuck. What would Papa say?

"Is it all right?" Ted asked anxiously. Then he said, rather crossly, "But it was *your* fault for grabbing my ball!"

"But *you* sat down on it!" Dai answered, as he worked at the lid.

The lock gave suddenly and the lid opened. The strings hung all awry. Then Dai saw that it was the bridge that had snapped. Everything else seemed intact, even the bow. He stood up with a sigh of thankfulness.

"Is it broken? *Is* it?" demanded Ted.

"Well, this is." Dai held up the little white wooden bridge in pieces. "But the case is really broken. I don't know what my father will say. He just gave it to me. . . . Well, I might as well go in and tell my mother. Then I'll have to see how to get the case fixed."

Dai gathered up his music, the fiddle, and the box and went into the house. The boys went back to their game.

Mama stood at the foot of the stairs. "What's the matter now? Your face is as long as a month of Sundays!"

Dai held out the broken fiddle case.

"Did you break your new fiddle?" Mama asked in a shocked voice.

"A little," said Dai, "but the case is *really* broken."

"How could you be so careless?" Mama scolded. "Even the case cost a good deal of money. It was not easy for Papa to get it for you."

"I know." Dai hung his head. "But only the bridge is broken on the fiddle. See?"

He took the violin out of the case and held it so Mama could see the limp strings and the little broken bridge.

"You will have to pay for the repair, you know. How much have you saved from your paper money?"

"Not very much."

"Papa can take it Monday to Mr. Moenig on Eleventh Street."

Dai nodded. He felt sick inside.

"You will have to buy a new bridge, too. Perhaps you aren't ready for that full-size violin after all."

When Papa came in from the matinee, Dai had to tell him about the fiddle case and the broken bridge. It was not easy.

Papa scowled as he examined the damage.

"You don't deserve to have this fine instrument! I thought you were old enough to treasure it and take care of it!"

Dai couldn't say a word. He gulped and tried to keep the tears back.

"I know. I was a boy once myself. I made a few mistakes, too. But you are going on twelve now. You *must* learn to be responsible for your own things and for yourself." Papa paused for a moment. Then he said, "Monday, I will take this in for repair. You will have to save your paper money to pay for it. I should think it will cost about two dollars. I hope it will be ready in time for the school concert. I'll try to get the bridge so you will have your fiddle for practice by Tuesday. I hope this will be a lesson to you!"

The evening of the school concert arrived. Dai was so happy that the repaired case and fiddle with its new bridge were ready for the occasion that he had practiced faithfully every day.

It was still daylight as he and Mama left for Heston school and most of the boys were playing in the street. Dai was in his best clothes.

"Hi!" called Ted, grinning. "Look at him! All dressed up!"

"Go to it!" yelled Butch. "Do a good job!" Dai pretended not to hear.

There was a buzz of excitement in the classroom where the performers were gathered with Miss Fraley, the music teacher. She wanted to make sure each one had his music ready.

When she asked Peter Androssi if he had everything he needed, he discovered his fiddle box was empty. He looked dismayed and Miss Fraley lost patience. "I suppose you left it just where you laid it down when you finished practicing this afternoon, didn't you?" She sighed. "Now what shall we do? There is no time for you to go home and get it. You are third on the program."

She turned to Dailey, asking with her look whether he would lend Peter his violin. Peter had no mother. His father did the best he could to look after Peter, who was absent-minded and careless about many things, although he played like an angel. If he remembered to bring his fiddle, he forgot the bow. If he remembered both, he forgot the music.

Dai knew he must lend Peter his violin, but he knew also that Peter's fingernails were long and not always clean. He hesitated, but what could he do? He loved Miss Fraley. He couldn't disappoint her and he was to be last on the program. He gave in.

"He can use my fiddle," he said, and handed it over.

Miss Fraley thanked him and Peter smiled gratefully, too shy to say anything.

The program began. Alice Newton played a Chopin prelude for the first number. Pretty good, thought Dai, as he listened near the door. Next, Mike Kowalsky played a lovely birdlike melody on the flute. Then, it was Peter's turn. He played Massenet's "Elegy," played it with such feeling that it brought wild applause from the audience. Much as he was moved by Peter's playing, Dai couldn't help being a little envious. It was *his* fiddle.

Peter bowed with old-fashioned grace, then lifted Dai's fiddle and played, as an encore, Dvorak's "Humoresque." On the very last note—PING! A string snapped! Dai gasped. His new fiddle!

27

But Mama, in the audience, held up her hand, waving a small package. She hurried to Dai, waiting in despair.

"Look!" she said. "I brought along some extra strings, just in case one might break." Peter came in just then as the applause was dying down and ruefully held out the violin with the hanging string. The other three strings were badly cut up, too, from Peter's long fingernails.

"I'm sorry," he said, "and thank you for your fiddle."

"Never mind," Mama said, "I brought all new strings, and you have time to put them on while the rest of the program goes on." Dai set to work.

Finally, it was Dai's turn. Miss Fraley played his accompaniment and all went well through the first pages.

Then, Dai lifted his eyes for a moment from the music and there in the front row sat two of the boys from the team, Ted and Chad.

Disaster struck. He lost the thread of the melody, fumbled for the right note, and stopped. He had to begin again.

Miss Fraley looked puzzled, but nodded her head and went back to the beginning. Dai was furious with himself.

This time he finished the piece without a mistake and bowed as he had been taught to do, from the waist.

The applause and the teacher's nod brought him to his senses. He lifted his fiddle and played the encore without missing a single note.

When Mama met him in the corridor after the concert, she didn't scold. She just put her arm around his shoulders and said, "Better luck next time. It's good that Papa wasn't here. You'll do better at the student recital and perhaps he will be home by then."

When Dai went for his next lesson, he met a boy with a fiddle case just coming out of the door.

"Hi!" he said, and the boy, passing, answered, "Hi!" He must be new, thought Dai. When he told Mr. Bucholz how he had failed at the school concert, and what had distracted him, the teacher said, "Keep your mind on your music and practice. I haff told you, yes? Be sure to practice and be ready for the student recital on Friday."

The student recital was given in Mr. Bucholz's parlor on Friday evening of the following week. Parents and friends were invited, so Mama and Grandma Craig asked Aunt Emily to join them. Aunt Emily still lived in Grandma de Angeli's house downtown at Tenth and Reed Streets. Dai could see them in the audience and wished Papa could have been there, too.

Dai played "My Heart Ever Faithful" by Bach, which he had been working on for weeks. He didn't miss a note and the pianissimo was, as Mr. Bucholz said, "smooth as silk."

After the recital, there was tea and cakes for the grownups and lemonade for the young people. Dai met a number of students he hadn't known before, one of them the boy who had passed him that day in the doorway. His name was Leon Arkless and he lived near Lancaster Avenue on Fortieth Street.

Dai said, "My name is Dailey de Angeli and I go to Heston school."

After that, they met several times at the studio.

Dai wished they lived nearer. It would be nice to have a friend who played the violin.

CHAPTER 3

One afternoon in early May when Dai came home from school, Papa was reading a letter to Mama as they sat over coffee in the kitchen.

"I'm expected to be there next weekend," Papa was saying. "Turner will take my place at Carncross's Saturday night, so we can stay overnight. Would you like that, Kate?" he said, and Dai wondered if he was remembering the summer when they had lost Danny.

"I think it would be fine," said Mama calmly.

Then Papa explained to Dai, "I have been asked to take charge of the entertainment on the new Steel Pier in Atlantic City, and to discuss the arrangements with the owner next Saturday. Would you like to go with Mama and me?"

"*Would* I? Wheeee!" He tossed his cap into the air. But what about the team? Who would pitch?

Papa went on. "You know sea air is very good for one's health. Perhaps it will be good for you, Kate, and you won't have so many fainting spells. Grandma Craig says she will take care of Roy, so we can leave early next Saturday morning. When you go for your lesson tomorrow, ask Mr. Bucholz to give you your lesson on Friday afternoon. I will talk to him."

"What shall I say to the team? The Red Lions are going to play the Pirates and I'm the pitcher."

"Oh, I'm sure they can find someone to pitch for you. How about that Chad I've heard you speak of?"

And that's how it turned out when Dai talked to Red Shafer.

"He'll do," said Red. "Chad's pretty good. When'll you be back?" He shifted his chewing gum.

"Oh, Sunday night, I s'pose. But my dad says maybe we might move down there after school is over. What then? Can I still be on the team till summer?"

"Oh, sure, we'll let you stay on." Red tapped his bat on his toe.

So it was settled.

When Dai went for his lesson on Friday he was surprised to see Leon there, too.

"It seems that both of you boys are going on a short holiday to Atlantic City. So, I arranged to teach you both at the same time today," said Mr. Bucholz.

"You too?" questioned Dai.

"Yes, my father is going down tomorrow to sign a contract to play in the Hotel Marlborough Blenheim for the summer." Leon was taking his fiddle out of the case and tuning it.

"That's funny, my father is going down to sign a contract to run the Minstrel Show on the Steel

Pier and hire bands for the summer. We're taking the train tomorrow."

"Me, too," said Leon, his chin hugging the chin rest on his violin.

"Goot, Goot! Now, let us begin," said Mr. Bucholz, sitting down at the piano. He turned around on the bench to remind the boys about keeping the measured beat of the andante of Schubert's "Ave Maria" by drawing the bow slowly over the strings. He "sshhed" them with one hand when the playing was too loud where it was marked pianissimo.

When the lesson was over, the boys agreed to meet in Atlantic City. Dai hurried home and into play clothes and to the lot to join the game. At least he could pitch until school was over.

Early on Saturday, Papa, Mama, and Dailey left for the seashore. It was a perfect May day.

They crossed by the ferry to Camden, where they took the train. For Dai, the trip through small Jersey towns was very exciting and he didn't want to miss anything. When they passed Absecon, the air became cooler and smelled of salt water. There were water birds standing long-legged in the marsh, ducks and geese that rose from the meadows to join the flocks of screaming gulls.

The train crossed a bridge over the Thorough-fare, a channel, very deep, between two inlets of the sea. It carved out bays and small harbors where Dai could see many fishermen.

Soon they arrived at the station. In 1898 Atlantic

City was a small seaside resort but was already well
known for its boardwalk. There were not many people this early in the season, but as they passed small
hotels and boardinghouses, windows were being
cleaned, people were putting chairs out on porches,
getting ready for vacationers.

Papa took them to a hotel near the beach, then

left for his appointment. Dai wondered where Leon was—Leon?—Arky? Yes, that was better. He thought he'd call him Arky. Perhaps he was staying with his parents at that big hotel, the Marlborough. Dai wished the summer had begun so Roy could be here. Then he and Arky could play on the beach, throw sticks into the water for Roy to retrieve.

While Mama was unpacking, Dai went out to explore on his own. There were only a few shops open on the boardwalk. He ran down onto the beach where gulls fluttered over the waves, following a school of fish. Two or three people down the beach seemed to be searching for something and every little while stooped to pick up something. What was it? As he passed the searchers he discovered they were picking up shells. Not just clam shells, oddly shaped ones. He began to look for them himself as he walked toward the big hotel, hoping that Arky would come out. *Arky,* he liked that.

Dai had been to the shore with Mama and Papa before, but had never noticed the different kinds of shells brought in by the tides. Now, he began looking, and soon found one different from those he had seen. It was washed white and clean but pitted with tiny holes as if it had been battered by the waves, Dai thought, but Mama would know about it.

He ran up onto the boardwalk again, hoping he would meet Arky.

There he was!

"Hi, Arky!" he called. "How do you like my new name for you?"

"Swell!" said Arky. "Where shall we go?"

"Let's hunt for shells, but after we have lunch. I'm getting hungry."

"So am I," Arky said.

"Okay. See you after lunch."

The boys were back together again as soon as lunch was over. They found razor shells, snail shells, and scallops to take home, where Mama identified them.

"I collected shells when I was a girl," she said, "but in all the changes in my life they have been scattered and lost. I still remember them and what they are called."

All of the two days they were in Atlantic City, Arky and Dai were together except for meals and bedtime. Soon, it was Sunday evening and time to go back to Philadelphia.

When Dai went for his next lesson, there was Arky just leaving.

"Hi!" he said. "How about it? Are you really going to be in Atlantic City this summer?"

"Yes, it's all settled. Dad goes down next week and we go as soon as school is out."

"Me too," said Arky delightedly. "My father goes right away and we're going to stay all summer. Won't it be great?"

"Great!" Dai agreed. "Now, I won't feel so sorry to leave the baseball team. I'm the pitcher. I guess they'll miss me this summer. I'll miss them, I know. Do you like baseball?"

"Sure! Don't you?"

"Of course. Doesn't everybody?" Dai gestured

with his arms, fiddle in one hand and music case in the other. "But they said Chad did pretty well last Saturday. I guess I'll miss them more than they will miss me. Oh, I must get up to the studio. By!" Dai ran up the stairs.

The days were almost as warm as summer, clear bright and beautiful. After school the boys played shinny stick, Duck on Davy, and, of course, baseball. They threw sticks for Roy to bring back, but one day Mama said, "You ask too much of that poor dog. Let him rest now."

Dai could hardly bear it when Mama called him in to practice. But there was one more lesson with Mr. Bucholz and, as she said, he must give a good account of himself.

As he played the familiar studies, Dai could hear the screeching and yelling, the pounding feet, the hooting laughter of the boys outside. He wondered what it would be like without his friends, especially Ted and Butch, who were in his class. Would there be any boys in the neighborhood where Papa had rented a house? He said it was in the part of Atlantic City called Chelsea, on Pacific Avenue.

When Dai went for his last lesson with Mr. Bucholz, Arky was still there, munching on a cooky Mrs. Bucholz had brought in.

"Hello, Arky, when do you go?" Dai asked. "My Dad has gone already."

When Arky had swallowed, and could speak, he grinned and said, "Next week. Our house is in

Chelsea. We rented it furnished. I think it is near that old church. Where's yours?"

"In Chelsea too! right on Pacific Avenue near California Street. Isn't that great! Only, we are moving down. My Dad thinks the sea air will be good for my mother."

"Come, Dai, time to get to work," said Mr. Bucholz.

"See you." Arky waved as he left. "Good-by, Mr. Bucholz."

"See you in Atlantic City," Dai called.

CHAPTER 4

At last mid-June came and the end of school. Dai
wondered what it would be like in another school.
Would he find friends there? He turned over his
paper route to Butch, who was glad to have it.
"Watch out for that old lady on Fifty-sixth Street,"
Dai said. "She bawled me out for whistling!" The
packing was finished and Papa came up from the
shore to help with the moving.

The boys stopped their ball game long enough to
watch the loading of the van, and when the family
left the house they all stood about soberly and
waved good-by. Dai hated to leave.

"Maybe I'll see you sometime again," he called,
walking backward. He carried his share of the luggage and kept hold of Roy's leash.

They stayed at the same hotel as before, only
now Grandma Craig was with them. Roy was left
at the new house where he could run in the yard
and Mama and Grandma went every day to clean
the house in readiness for the furniture. Papa
helped when he could and Dai worked harder than
he ever had in his life, carrying out trash from the
cellar and burning it, putting bottles and jars in

baskets in the alley to be collected. He even washed windows and polished them till they sparkled.

The furniture arrived and Dai thought how different everything looked. When Mama made up his bed in the new room, he felt as if it must be for someone else. The oval-backed sofa looked like new where it stood in the parlor. Great-grandfather Benedict and his niece, Beatrice de Angeli, who had come to this country in 1830, seemed very stately in their old-fashioned dress. The portraits had been painted by Bass Otis and because they hung in a new place and different light, Dai noticed them and thought, Why they were real people and I belong to them! But if it hadn't been for *you*, I wouldn't have to practice all the time. He made a face at Benedict.

The next morning Dai was free to look for Arky. But he had hardly left the house when they met.

They joined forces and went exploring, first to the boardwalk to examine the scene from this new angle. Roy greeted Arky with a wag of his tail. Arky patted him as they walked along sniffing the fresh cool air of June at the shore.

There were all kinds of catch-penny shops along the boardwalk: ice cream parlors, candy stores with great ropes of gleaming salt water taffy turning on candy-pulling machines, and fudge shops with trays of tempting chocolate squares, and in front of a barbershop, a parrot hung in a cage. As the boys stopped to look at him, he croaked, "Hello, darling. Hello, darling!" Very embarrassing, but funny.

There were a number of people passing, stopping to look in the windows, some leaning on the guardrail overlooking the beach and the ocean. Others relaxed in rolling chairs pushed by attendants, already a famous Atlantic City attraction.

After lunch the boys met again and raced down to the beach, but this time, far down where there were no people, only sandpipers and gulls, driftwood and shells. An old surf boat lay swamped at the edge of the water where ripples washed around it. The boys stripped down to their underclothes and dived into the water.

"Brr-rr-rr! It's *cold!*" shouted Dai. They'd soon had enough, but Roy didn't mind. He had his fur coat on. The boys dressed and warmed themselves by running in the sand, throwing sticks for Roy to retrieve. He was enjoying it as much as they were. Suddenly, he tired and lay down in the sun. It seemed a good idea. The boys lay down beside him until they caught their breath.

Excitement took them back to the boardwalk, where there were interesting shops they hadn't seen.

One store front held a sign—"Fortunes Told. Come in and hear the future."

"Do you suppose they really *can?*" asked Dai.

"Aw, that's silly," answered Arky, as they wandered on. Another place had a sign saying, "Come in and see the fattest woman in the world!! See the smallest man!" The boys peered in the window, but there was nothing but darkness.

Dai thought he would like to see the smallest man in the world. What would he be like?

Just then, the door opened and out he walked! The smallest man in the world! At least, he was the smallest man Dai had ever seen. He walked out just as any man would, going his own way and paying no attention to the two boys who stared at him. How could he eat at table? thought Dai. How could he get into a chair, or board a trolley car, or reach a counter in a store? The boys looked at each other in awe.

When Dai told Mama about the tiny man, she said, "I hope you didn't stare at him. He can't help being different from most men. There are many differences among people, but each person has his place in the world. Don't forget that."

"Oh, I won't. I just thought he was interesting, like a person in a fairy tale."

Several days later when the boys were hunting clams, they met another boy whose name was El-mer. He was a little younger than either Dai or Arky.

"Want to help us dig clams?" Dai asked. "My mother wants to make clam chowder, a kind of soup."

"Ssthure. My mother make-th thoup, too," he said, and the boys roared with laughter.

"Well, shthee dothe," he went on, frowning. "Whatth tho funny, hunh?"

"The way you talk," Dai said. "But that-th O.K.," he laughed. "You're a good guy anyway. Want to come along with us this afternoon?" Elmer nodded his agreement but didn't speak for fear the boys would laugh again.

Each morning after that first day at the shore, Dailey woke up thinking, "No practice!" What would happen today? What would he and Arky find to do? There were errands to do for Mama, clams to dig on the beach or in the meadows; there were fish to be caught in the Thoroughfare; and once in a while, the Minstrel Show.

Dai was forbidden to hang about the Pier, but sometimes he and Arky stood near the entrance to listen to the band, which was just inside. Papa engaged famous conductors, such as Victor Herbert, Sousa, and others, to attract people to the Pier. He also had a smaller orchestra to play for the Minstrel Show.

On the next street near the bay, there was a livery stable where Dai liked to go. He made friends with Frank, the young man who worked there, by offering to help him one day.

"Can I give you a hand?" he called to Frank as he was trying to move a small carriage with a broken axle.

"You sure can! Give that off wheel there a boost. Then I can get it over here. I've got to make a new part on the swage, but I gotta have it nearer."

Dai lifted his end of the carriage enough so that Frank could shift it into position to work on it. After that, Frank showed Dai how many things operated. The swage was a tool on which metal could be worked without heating. It was used for shaping or forming metal objects, such as the head on a bolt.

Sometimes Dai helped Frank groom the ponies that little children rode on the beach, or watched while he mended harness. Frank answered Dai's questions and took the trouble to explain how and why he did things.

Near the bay and not far from the livery stable Dai discovered the city dump, where all kinds of useful things could be found. Before long he had quite a collection of treasures in the basement— driftwood boards, whitened by the weather and the sea, a jew's-harp, a hammer head with no handle, empty jars, in case one had something to put in them, such as nails or screws. There were ends of rope, and a pair of ladies' high-button shoes.

When Dai brought in the shoes, Mama laughed. "What on earth are you going to do with ladies' shoes?"

"I'm going to wear them to the President's ball!"

Mama laughed again.

Dai went on down to the basement. "You never know when you might need a good piece of leather," he called back.

One day he found the base of a baby carriage, wheels and all. "Oh, boy! Can I make a cart out of that!" Except for Roy, Dai usually made these expeditions alone. How could he share such treasures? By the time he had dragged the thing home, he had it all planned how to make the cart. "I could even put a sail on it and let the wind carry me along. It will be fun to make it all by myself and show it to Arky and Elmer." It began to rain. Just the kind of day to work inside.

"What have you got there?" Mama asked as he dragged the wheel base through the kitchen to the basement door. "More junk?" She turned her head to see. Grandma Craig chuckled.

"What that boy doesn't think of." She winked at Dai as he opened the door.

"Something you're going to help me with," he said over his shoulder, his voice diminishing as he went down the stairs, dragging his find.

I can use the tools from Papa's new tool box, he thought. Papa had said he might use them if he was careful, but he cautioned Dai they must be put back in place.

All morning he was sawing and hammering, making a boxlike top for the base. He fastened it to the base with two pieces of board cut from the driftwood and joined to the top by passing them under the metal frame.

"Could you make me a sail?" he asked Mama. "I could sail down the boardwalk in the wind. Wouldn't *that* be fun! Could you?"

"I think I could. I'll look and see what I have."

Mama found an old muslin sheet, cut it to the size Dai wanted, then double-stitched it along the edges to strengthen it. She even gave Dai one of her clothesline props for a mast. Fastening the mast to the cart was a problem. Then Dai remembered the leather in the high-topped shoes. He cut them into strips and reinforced the joint by wrapping the strips around the mast and tacking them down. It didn't occur to him that it might be difficult to get the cart and mast out of the cellarway. It was.

He had hardly started up the stairs when he realized his mistake.

"HELP!" he called, and it took the assistance of both Mama and Grandma to get the contraption out of the cellar. There it was, when Papa came home, all ready to go.

"That's pretty good craftsmanship, son."

Dai was happy that Papa had liked his handiwork. Papa enjoyed working with tools himself, but had little time for it.

Dai could hardly wait for morning to try the sail-wagon. The rain had stopped and right after breakfast, he was out with his invention and on his way to Arky's. Elmer was already there and they had planned to play ball, expecting Dai to play, too. They admired the sail-wagon, but their minds were set for baseball. Much as Dai loved baseball, he wanted *now* to ride the sail-wagon.

"It's great!" said Arky, swinging his bat back and forth. "But only one can ride, right?"

"I think it-th thwell," Elmer said, punching his hand into the baseball mitt.

It seemed to Dai that neither of the boys appreciated his sail-wagon as much as he had thought they would. He loved to play ball, but today, he would rather sail down the boardwalk in the brisk wind with Roy racing beside him.

Arky and Elmer looked somewhat crestfallen as Dai left them and turned toward the sea. He had to push the wagon with his foot on the sidewalk, but when he reached the boardwalk, the cart was off. The sail caught the wind and Dai felt as if he were really sailing and captain of his own ship. "Ahoy!"

Roy ran happily beside him as fast as he could go with his three-skip-one, three-skip-one.The wind carried the sail-wagon along the boardwalk, past the shops, the bathing houses, the grand hotels. It was a glorious ride. Dai lifted his head to watch the waves roll in and glimpse the far horizon where sea met the sky. Then—PLOP! Down they went. They had sailed off the end of the boardwalk. Rip went the sail, crack went the mast, and that was the end of the sail-wagon.

The cart was still whole, Dai discovered when he had shaken the sand out of his eyes and had seen that Roy was not hurt. Then he thought about Mama. Would she faint when she saw them?

Not this time. She laughed at the sight of Dai, his hair sticking up, full of sand, and at the trail of crunching sand Dai and Roy left on the kitchen floor.

"Well," she said, "you must have gone off the deep end. I'll have to wash your hair and your ears. Get Roy out of here. We'll take care of him later. I'm glad your cart can still be used."

Even though Dai considered this vacation time, Mama had decided that he must practice a half-hour each evening. "It's no fair," he said, pouting. But when Mama suggested that he play the old songs instead of scales, he felt better. It was fun to play the Scottish ballads for Grandma Craig. She so enjoyed them. She even joined Mama in singing sometimes. Her voice was quavery, but sweet. Dai learned to love the old songs, too, and it helped his sight reading.

One night when Papa came home, he heard Dai playing.

"You know, son," he said, "I think you could substitute for a young violinist in the orchestra who wants to go to his sister's wedding tomorrow night. I'm sure Victor Herbert will be glad to have you. I told him you could read the score and that you would like to do it for him. You would, wouldn't you?"

"Whoooo! *Me?* I'll try, but I have only played with students, you know."

"I know, but you will have to start sometime. You'll play second fiddle, of course. Mr. Herbert may need you to play a solo, too. What could you play?"

"I know 'My Heart Ever Faithful' pretty well. Will that do? And do I have to have an encore?"

"You'd better have one ready," Mama said. "How about the 'Traumerei'? You play that well and it is not too long."

"Yes, that will do very well. I will count on you, and so will Mr. Herbert."

Next morning Mama said, "You can do a half-hour's sight reading before you go with the boys. I hear them out in the yard playing with Roy. I'll tell them to go on to the beach and take him along and when you have finished practicing, you can join them." Dai sighed and got out his violin. It was a beautiful day and he longed to be out on the beach with the others.

Finally, his time was up. Mama let him go and he ran all the way, pulling the cart. There might be driftwood.

Roy was always wild with joy when the boys took him to the beach. He seemed to know that the game of retrieving sticks was on the way and when they were thrown into the surf, he brought them back, dripping and proud, his eyes shining. Over and over, he raced into the water and back again.

That afternoon, when the waves were rough, and they had been playing for some time, Dai threw a large piece of driftwood with all his might out into the boiling surf.

"Bet he can't find *this* one!" Out it sailed over the breaking waves and was lost for a moment in a foaming tumble of water with Roy after it. He swam strongly at first. Then, when he couldn't see the stick for the frothy waves he began to falter. The boys stood watching with suddenly anxious looks. They saw Roy carried over a breaker. They saw him for a brief moment lying quite still on the water. Then—he was gone.

"Oh, oh," Dai cried, "he's caught in the under-tow," and he raced into the surf after Roy, sobbing as he fought his way through incoming breakers. He found Roy as he came to the surface once again and gathered him close.

The boys helped to lift him from Dai's arms as he walked out of the water and laid him on the sand.

Dai worked frantically over Roy, rubbing his back and legs, talking to him, hugging him, trying to get him to breathe.

But it was too late.

The boys wept bitterly over the beloved dog as he lay on the sand.

What would they do without Roy?

"He always did whatever we asked him to," sobbed Dai as he hugged Roy to himself.

"He was the best dog I ever saw," said Arky solemnly.

"He could do more on three legths than any dog with four legths," Elmer sniffed.

"If only I hadn't kept throwing sticks," mourned Dai. "My mother told me I tired him out too much. I wish I had listened." He shivered in his wet clothes.

"C'mon, we'd better get home."

Together, they lifted Roy onto the cart, pulled it out of the sand, over the dunes to the sidewalk. Only now Roy was not skipping beside them. They took him into the back yard just as Mama opened the door.

She knew immediately that something was wrong. "What happened?" she questioned. Then she saw the limp body on the cart with the boys standing guard beside him.

"Poor Roy, poor old friend," she said, looking at Dai, sadly. He couldn't keep the tears back.

"Now," she continued, "it's too late to bury Roy tonight, so get out of those wet clothes. Take your bath." Arky and Elmer left quietly.

"Dailey," Mama said, "put on your good suit so you will be ready for tonight. Then, you'd better practice while I get dinner."

"How can I play when Roy is gone?" Dai mourned.

"Practice will take your mind off your troubles," Mama said, laying her hand comfortingly on Dai's head. "If you really think about your music and play as well as you possibly can, it will comfort you. And tonight remember that you are helping Papa. Think, too, about the pleasure you are giving others. It always helps us to do something for some-one else. Remember?"

Dai nodded, and went upstairs.

When he came down, dressed and ready for the evening, Papa was home.

Dai's grief welled up again, but Papa put his arm around Dai's shoulders and said, "I know how terribly you will miss Roy, son, but we keep the memory of all we loved about our friends and they continue to live in our thoughts. Some day, you will have another dog. He will be different and he won't be Roy, but you will be just as fond of him."

"Oh, I could never love another dog as much as Roy." Dai shook his head and went toward the parlor to practice. Papa's voice followed him.

"We'll see. Tomorrow, you boys can take Roy down the beach and bury him in the dunes he loved."

Dai took his fiddle out of the box and began to tune it. He went over and over the piece he was to play on the Pier.

As Mama had said, the lovely melody of "Trau-merei" was comforting, though sad. The very mo-tion of the bow over the vibrating strings was soothing.

That evening, Dai played as he had never played before. He remembered to play it andante as he had been taught, with the turn gently even and the accents in the proper places. He thought to himself, "I played almost as well as Peter." He was surprised to see Mr. Bucholz and his wife in the audience, although he knew they often came to the shore for a weekend.

After the show, Mr. Bucholz came to congratulate Dai on his playing. He put his hand on Dai's shoulder and shook his hand as if he'd been grown up.

"Fine, fine, my son," he said, and again, "Fine! Some day you vill make them all laugh and cry, iss it not?" Then he nodded his head and closed his eyes. "I know, I know," he said, and Dai knew he was saying how sorry he was about Roy. Papa must have told him.

As they walked home, Papa kept his arm around Dai's shoulders. "I'm very proud of you and the way you played tonight," he said. "Mr. Herbert spoke to me about it. Perhaps you can play again on the Pier."

Next morning, Arky, Elmer, and Dailey took Roy to bury him.

They wrapped him in the piece of sheeting Mama had made for the sail-wagon and took him on the cart, out the back gate, down to the boardwalk to the very end. The dunes stood bleak and wind-swept under the cloudy sky.

"Where shall we bury him?" asked Arky mournfully.

"Up there on the top would be a good place, where the sea can't reach. He can't swim now." Dai was very near to tears.

"He wath tho nithe," sighed Elmer.

The boys dragged the cart up through the sand to the top of the dune and began to dig the grave.

Long grass with deep roots in the sand made it hard to dig, so the boys took turns with Papa's shovel, digging deep and sniffing sadly as they worked.

When the grave was deep enough, the three of them lifted Roy's body gently and they buried him. Dai found a small board washed up on the beach and with his penknife carved Roy's name on it.

The boys didn't feel like doing anything, not even playing ball. They walked slowly down the beach, hardly speaking, their heads down.

CHAPTER 5

The next day seemed without purpose or interest to either Dai or Arky and when Elmer joined them to play ball on the lot near the lighthouse, he said, "It theemths funny without Roy, doethen't it?" The other boys just nodded. They played listlessly at first, but the exercise caught their attention and they tossed and batted the ball around all afternoon.

When Papa had come home and they were all at dinner, he looked around the table and, seeing everyone's sad looks, said brightly, "I'll tell you what—let's all go to the Minstrels tonight. I've just taken on a new man, Gus Bruno. He's very funny and I think he will cheer you up. And, Kate, if you are willing, we could let him stay here for a few days. He's not young and has been out of work for a long time, so he has no money till he is paid. Perhaps he could sleep on the couch. Do you think we can manage to have him?"

"Of course," Mama agreed. "We'll manage. I can give him his meals, too, if that will help."

"I saw him once some years ago in Chicago. I don't know how tidy he will be," Papa warned. "But

I will try to see that this doesn't make too much trouble for you."

Papa was very particular about how the company looked. He always dressed immaculately and it was a part of the show that all the performers wore knee breeches, a frilled shirt and white gloves. Once in a while when Dai attended the show he sat on Papa's make-up trunk and watched while Papa put on the paint that changed him from Papa into an actor.

It was always friendly backstage. Dai knew all the permanent actors, those who stayed all summer, such as Vic Richards, Frank Tinney, and Hughey Dougherty. The others changed from week to week. There were no women in the show, but wives often accompanied their husbands while they were at the shore. They lived in lodgings or small hotels. Sometimes Mama invited them for dinner, or, on Sundays, they went "offshore" for a picnic. Offshore meant across the meadows by trolley car to Pleasantville or Absecon, where there was cool shade in the woods.

Dai loved the actors' jokes and sense of fun and wished he might go to the show more often.

Gus Bruno proved to be just as funny as Papa said. Dai had thought that after Roy was gone he would never feel like laughing again. But at every mealtime Gus Bruno told such funny stories, Dai laughed with the others, and thought nothing could be better than to make people laugh, traveling all over the country as actors did and as Papa did. But when he spoke about it to Gus Bruno, he said, "Do something else, lad. It's the hardest life in the world. One day you are rich, or you *think* you are, and the next, you wonder where you will sleep or where you will find a meal.

"Sometimes you need a sense of humor to get you through. People are funny. They are like sheep. They will follow anybody who looks as if he knows where he is going.

"Why, one day, I was just wandering around without a job when an idea struck me. I wondered what would happen if I looked up. There were plenty of people around because it was noontime. So I just stood still and looked up at the sky. I hadn't been looking up but a few seconds when people began to stop and look up, too. I pretended to take something out of my pocket and dropped it onto the pavement. Then I made believe I was mixing something and kept looking up, then down. People kept gathering till there was quite a crowd. Then I took a match out of my pocket, lighted it, and dropped it where it could do no harm, and I ran. Do you know, all those silly people ran after me for blocks! Finally, I had to stop because I was out of breath and I had quite a time explaining things to a policeman!"

Gus Bruno gestured as he talked and his swift-changing expression brought the people in his stories to life.

Dai could hardly wait to tell Arky and Elmer about Gus Bruno and his funny stories. It was sad about Roy but they couldn't mourn him forever. It would do them all good to have a laugh.

"There was this German who spoke broken English and was poor," Dai began. "He belonged to a troupe traveling around the country. They stayed at a hotel and arrived just before breakfast. When the waiter asked the German how he would like his eggs—boiled or fried?—the German said, 'I'll take fife!'" The boys laughed as Dai had hoped. Then he went on, "Another time an actor who thought he was SOMEBODY, but who was penniless as many of them were, said to the waiter, 'I'm not very hungry. Just bring me some tea and toast.' Gus Bruno said to him, 'Why not have dinner? The company's paying for it.' 'They *are?*' said the actor, rubbing his hands together, 'WELL, that's different! I'll take everything on the menu from soup to nuts!'"

Dai laughed as hard as the other boys.

At the end of the week, Gus Bruno left the house and took a room somewhere. Dai wished he could stay on, but Mama said, "Enough's enough!"

Dai guessed that Mama didn't like funny men as much as he did, and he had to admit that it was pleasant not to see Mr. Bruno in his nightshirt on the couch at lunchtime.

"But where did that gun come from?" he asked Mama, as she tidied up after Mr. Bruno had gone.

"Well, Mr. Bruno gave it to Papa to make up for his staying here," said Mama. "I don't like guns. But Papa says that when he has time he will take you to the meadows to teach you how to use it properly, and maybe shoot ducks. Mind you, don't touch it. Papa will show it to you."

When Papa came home, Dai could hardly wait till he sat down to ask about the gun. He brought it from the kitchen and begged Papa to show him how it worked. Mama stood by looking doubtful.

"It's a sixteen-gauge, double-barreled Parker shotgun," Papa began, smoothing the wooden stock. He lifted the lock and opened the breech to show the mechanism and how the gun was loaded. Then Papa held Dai by his arms and looked straight into his eyes.

"This gun is for you when you are twelve, but you are not to touch this gun until I can go with you and teach you how to use it properly. *Understand?*"

He emphasized what he was saying by giving Dai's arms a tight squeeze, then said, "We will stand the gun here in the corner where you can see it and know that it will be yours." Dai nodded his agreement, then threw his arms around Papa's neck.

"Come now," Mama said, "Grandma's waiting, supper's ready."

Papa rose, taking the gun with him, stood it carefully in the corner, and said, "Remember!" And they went in to supper.

Dai looked longingly at the shiny barrel of the gun and wished his twelfth birthday had been today instead of months away, but, he thought, "Maybe he will take me shooting one of these days, anyway."

It was now late June, but many days were cool, the water, icy cold. The boys liked to wander over the meadows to Cap Brockway's boat yard, where sail- and rowboats were repaired and painted and where they were laid up for the winter.

At first, Captain Brockway kept a close eye on the boys, cautioning them not to handle tools nor climb aboard the boats. But Dai promised they would not touch anything and soon Captain Brockway learned to trust them even when Elmer was with them. He was patient with their questions, allowing the boys to watch as he worked, explaining the use and need for stays to hold the mast and other rigging. He joked with them, sometimes shared his lunch with them, and let them be "gofors"—go for the hammer, go for the chisel, go for the mail.

He was their friend.

One day, taking his pipe out of his mouth, he said, "How would you like to go fishing? There's an old rowboat you can use and I've got some fishin' tackle I'll lend you. But mind, you must stay near the shore of this cove so I can hear you if you holler." He looked earnestly into Dai's eyes and at Arky to make sure he could trust them. Their straight looks reassured him.

"Can you both swim?" he asked as he went for the oars and the tackle.

"Oh, yes, we can swim," both boys answered at once, each taking his share of things to carry across to the edge of the cove where the boat lay.

She was an old tub of a boat, waterlogged and heavy to manage, but she changed things for Arky and Dai. They stayed in the cove as Cap Brockway had cautioned them and sometimes made a good catch of weakfish or bass. Sometimes they sat for hours in the broiling sun and caught nothing. Once in a while Elmer went with them, but he couldn't swim and his mother seldom allowed him to go.

One day, Dai and Arky caught nothing. The air was so still, the sun so hot, they began to find fault with each other. At first, it was more in fun than in earnest.

"We've drifted almost to the other side of the cove. Why did you insist on going this side of the boat yard? I wanted to go the other side." Dai pointed.

"You did *not!*" Arky came back. "Besides, you never gave me back that nickel I loaned you." He pulled with all his might on the oars, but it seemed that the rowboat hardly moved.

"I did *too!* I gave it to you when you bought that candy at the fudge place. I know, 'cause my mother asked me if I gave it to you. So there!" Um*mnh!* Dai too strained at his oar, trying to outdo Arky.

"Well, you ate more than your share of it. I hardly had any."

"If you weren't such a pig, you wouldn't even notice." Dai made a face at Arky, who returned the compliment. "Just wait till I get you on shore!" he said, "I'll show you who's a pig! You play the fiddle like a pig too 'cause you don't practice enough."

"I do *so* practice anyway, I've played in the or- chestra. *You* never did!" With a spurt of energy, Dai tried his best to send the boat toward land, but she hardly moved.

The argument went on, far afield from the way it had begun.

Suddenly they discovered the light had changed. The sun had an eerie look. Black clouds had gathered in the west and a storm was brewing. The wind too was rising, beginning with a low murmur, growing in sound and fury by the moment.

With one accord and not a word said, looking as threatening as the black sky over them, each took up an oar. Furiously they dipped the oars deep and started rowing, angrily, jerkily, each determined to outdo the other.

Leaves and twigs flew past in the wind. They tugged and pulled. Harder and harder, as if life depended on their haste, they finally reached the dock, exhausted and breathless.

When they tried to ship the oars, they could scarcely raise them above the water. And no wonder!

The oars were loaded with what seemed like a ton of seaweed.

That broke the ice. The boys doubled up with laughter, all sour looks gone. Friendship was restored.

As thunder roared and lightning flashed, Cap Brockway came to see what was causing all the merriment.

When their laughter had subsided somewhat, the boys slipped the line over the mooring and dived into the water to cool off.

A sharp flash of lightning warned them to come

out of the water and they took refuge in Cap Brockway's workshop until the storm was over.

After that day, the boys rather lost interest in the old rowboat.

For one thing, Mama insisted that Dailey begin regular practice again. She said he must work at it for a half-hour before going out with the boys and an hour in the afternoon, in addition to playing for her and Grandma Craig in the evening.

"You are getting lazy," she scolded one morning. "You've had enough vacation. You know the old saying—'Slothfulness shall suffer hunger.' You don't want to be hungry, do you?"

"What's *sloth*fulness? I never heard of it."

"You know perfectly well it's laziness. Get to work." Mama smiled, rubbed his hair the wrong way, and left.

The practice hour seemed long on bright days. Yet as he played, Dai felt that the whole world seemed to expand as if it had been a great colored ball and he a part of it. It was a kind of glory, and as if he were free of the earth and high above it. At other times, the music gave him a feeling of deep sadness, not unbearable sadness, just sorrow for people who didn't care for music. He wondered whether Arky felt that way, but wouldn't think of asking. Arky, too, had to practice in the afternoons. He played on and on till Arky came to the door.

They took bat and ball down to the beach, dressed for swimming as the day was warm. Elmer met them at the corner. "What-th doin'?" he said, and joined them. The beach was crowded with vacationers and excursionists, so the boys wandered down past houses and shops and began to look for shells. Dai picked up a strange-looking string of pouchlike things connected by a leathery strand.

"Look at this funny thing!" he cried. Elmer came up with his hands full. Dai shook the thing, which rattled, and out of small holes in each pouch, tiny, tiny shells dropped. They were perfectly formed and were like the large one they had found early in the summer. "Exthquithite!" declared Elmer.

Arky, too, had a handful of treasures, an angel wing and a whelk with a pink lining and knobs around the crown, very much like the tiny ones, but more colorful. Elmer's handful of shells were mostly scallops. Only he said, "Thcallopth."

When the boys showed Mama their collections she said, sighing, "Many's the one I've found. I wish I'd kept them all. But when you've moved as many times as I have, you get tired of packing things. So, I gave this one away, then that one, and first thing you know, there weren't any left. I'm glad you boys are finding them again. That large one with the pink lining is a whelk. That long string of pouches is an egg case of the whelk. That's an angel wing, and those are scallops." The boys nodded. Each took his own treasures to keep.

CHAPTER 6

One morning when it was too cool to enjoy swimming, and there seemed nothing worth-while doing, Mama suggested that Dai and Arky go in search of clams in the meadows. She gave them a trowel and small basket to carry them in. "Remember," she said, "that the birds' nests are all over the ground. You must go carefully so as not to disturb them and be sure to put seaweed on top of the clams to keep them cool and moist."

"Seaweed?" said Dai, making a face, "I never want to see any again. I've had my fill of seaweed. Remember?"

"Yes, I remember," Mama nodded, "but it will take only a little to keep the clams fresh, not a *ton*."

Dai and Arky started out toward the meadows. They met Elmer on the way and said he could go with them.

"Justh wait till I tell my mother," he called over his shoulder as he ran toward home.

"Bring a basket for clams!" yelled Dai. Elmer nodded and was soon back with a basket.

They started out toward the meadows, past the scattered houses, the little farm where geese came to the fence honking defiance.

"Honk! honk, yourself!" Dai poked his finger
through the fence and nearly had it nipped. For a
few minutes it was fun to tease the geese, then the
boys went on out to the meadows where blue heron
were feeding along the marshes and white egrets
stood looking for frogs. Hundreds of gulls and terns
wheeled about. Several varieties of duck swam in

pools or nested on the hummocks. The birds, great and small, flew up in alarm as the boys invaded their territory, then settled down again as the boys dug for clams in the marshy ground. They saw little fiddler crabs scramble for shelter and, as Mama had cautioned them, stepped around nests of eggs shining white in the sun. They soon had their baskets filled, and added a few crabs caught in the shallow water.

Arky discovered an arrowhead and a great pile of oyster shells.

"Maybe there were Indians here," he said excitedly, as they examined the ancient arrowhead. "Yeah—Indians."

"*Ind*ianth? Wow!"

As they moved on to look for more treasures, the ground gave way to a small stream, and there, through the long grass, Dai spied an abandoned boat. It had no oars, though there were oarlocks, and no mast, though there was a place for one, and it was filled with rushes. A somewhat ragged sail lay across the cockpit. Wonder who left it? thought Dai.

"Hey!" he yelled to Arky and Elmer, who were still searching for arrowheads.

"Look! I've found a boat. It doesn't belong to anybody, 'way out here in the meadows. It's been here for years. Let's take it back to the Thoroughfare. Maybe we can have it for keeps. We can even rig a sail on it." Dai was already testing it for movability.

They tried to push the derelict into the stream

where the rushes bent with the flow of the water. It was hard work getting it out of the tall grass where it was grounded, but finally they made it by pushing and pulling. Since there were no oars, the boys had to wade and drag the boat. When the water became too deep, Dai swam, pushing it, while Arky and Elmer pulled from the bank. It was a long haul to Cap Brockway's boat yard, but at last, they made it.

Cap Brockway assured them they could have the boat. "But," he cautioned, "she's waterlogged and heavy, so she's not easy to manage. It will take quite a lot of work to get her in shape. The tiller is broken, you'll have to fix that. If you've got any tools, better bring 'em. I need mine."

"Well, let's see what we can find." He moved off toward the shop, the boys following. He found yards of rope, a piece of what had been a large sail, and a discarded pair of oars. The rope was tar-soaked and in pieces, but Cap Brockway showed them how to splice it as sailors did. The sail was already patched and torn in some places. "But your Ma can fix that," he said.

"You can find a young cedar or a length of ash for mast and for boom and gaff. This sneak box will need a mast about sixteen feet high and a boom about nine feet, and a gaff about seven." Meantime, Cap Brockway was moving papers around to find a picture showing the missing parts, what they were for and how they would be used. Arky and Dai listened carefully to the instructions. Elmer leaned against the work table.

"Show your ma this, so she will know what to do. I think I can find hoops somewhere around here. You boys can sew those on here in the shop. When you get these things together, bring 'em here and I'll help you step the mast and rig her." Cap Brockway went on with his work, then continued, "Now, you know, sailing is serious business. I *won't* help you unless you *promise* to *stay in this cove* and within hailing distance. This old tub won't go very fast, but a sudden squall and you're sunk. Heavy as she is, she could overturn."

Suddenly Elmer said, "I got to go home. I'm hungry."

"Me, too," said Arky, and they all picked up their baskets of smelly clams and started home. "I'll see you after lunch," Dai called. "We'll go to the woods below Chelsea to find the cedar mast and boom and gaff."

He enjoyed using the nautical words.

"What kept you? I began to worry," Mama said, taking the basket, "And WHAT IS THAT?"

"Guess what! We've got a real boat! It's going to be a sailboat." He dropped the heavy sail onto the floor and spread it out. "Look! Can you mend it?" Mama nodded. "Here's the directions for how to do it."

"I think so," she said. "I can put double cloth over the holes. I think my machine will stitch through this heavy cloth so I can hem it." She gathered up the sail and put it aside.

"Come now, your lunch has been waiting for a long time."

It didn't take any coaxing. Dai was hungry. Grandma Craig began sorting the clams, removing the sticks and leaves. While Dai was eating, he told about all their adventures, the interesting things they had found, the arrowheads and the great mound of oyster shells.

"Why were they there, I wonder," said Dai. "There were tons of them."

"Oh, the Indians left those," said Mama. "The Lenapes used to come down here in the summer from Pennsylvania and New Jersey to find clams and oysters to dry for the winter and, of course, they left piles of shells behind them."

"*Real* Indians? Think of it!" Dai gazed out of the window, imagining how the Indians must have looked with their blankets and moccasins, their feathers and neck chains, just as he had seen in pictures. Then he came back to the finding of the boat and how they had pushed and pulled it to Cap Brockway's wharf and he had said they could keep it. And now they were to go to the woods to find timbers for rigging.

"But isn't it dangerous for you boys to have a sailboat?" Mama said anxiously, as she began to think about it, remembering her lost Daniel.

"Oh, no, it's not dangerous. Arky and I can swim like anything and we promised to stay where Cap Brockway could hear us if we holler."

Grandma Craig looked up from the clams she was sorting.

"How about Elmer? His ma won't let him go, will she?"

"Oh, I guess she will," said Dai, still chewing. "He can swim a little. Anyway, Arky and I will look after him."

Before Dai had finished eating, Arky and Elmer were at the gate calling for him. "Wait till I get the hatchet!" he shouted.

"Don't stay too late," Mama called from the door-way. "And be careful."

"We will," Dai called as he ran out after the other boys.

The woods, where the boys had been exploring before, was quite a way below Chelsea. Mama called after them, "Remember to be careful! That is not your property, you know. Take only what is lying on the ground!"

"We will!" Dai called back.

The land was undeveloped with woods, scrub oak, and cedar trees. A sign had been posted—DO NOT LIGHT FIRES NOR CUT DOWN TREES.

"It-th' fun in the woodth," said Elmer, as they wandered through the prickly undergrowth, kicking up dead leaves. Beneath were all kinds of tiny growing plants, fresh and crisp, pipsissewa, winter-green, and ground pine. There were bushes of laurel, too, the flowers now fading.

Of course the boys didn't know what the plants were called, but they ate the fragrant wintergreen berries and wondered at the living things beneath the carpet of dead leaves.

"I'm glad we left the cart at the edge of the woods," Dai said. "We could hardly get it through here. Ouch! These prickly branches hurt."

They found plenty of dead trees lying about, but even after they had chopped off the branches, it wasn't easy to get them out to the cart.

The boys worked hard. Dai kept the hatchet in his own hands. It belonged to Papa. When they had gathered the poles they needed and tied them onto the cart, they dropped to the needle-strewn ground for a rest.

"I'm bushed," Dai sighed, as he tossed the hatchet into the cart.

"Unh-huh, me too." Arky stretched his length on the ground.

"Tho'm I!" Elmer joined him.

A few moments of rest seemed to be enough. Dai sat up.

"I'm hungry," he said. "Let's go home."

Then began the business of getting the trees onto the cart, balanced and tied on so they would stay put. It was finally managed and the boys trudged toward the meadows. Elmer left them at the street where he lived. Arky went on with Dai to help him get the cartload to the boat yard. It was a long way back and Cap Brockway had gone for the night, so the boys laid the poles beside the shed and started home.

There wasn't much conversation on the way back. Both boys were tired out, but now they were really on the way to having their very own sailboat.

"Well," Mama greeted Dai as he dragged himself into the kitchen, "you've been gone a long time. It's a good thing you get hungry. How about that practicing you were going to do?"

Dai just shook his head wearily.

Papa came in.

"What's up?" he queried. When he saw Dai's weary figure at the kitchen table, he said, "What have you been doing? You look all in!"

"Oh, just getting a mast for our boat," Dai said.

"*Your boat?*" questioned Papa.

Then the whole story had to be told again.

When Papa heard about finding the boat and how Cap Brockway was helping the boys rig her and would be on the lookout for them, he nodded his head in agreement. "Well, I guess it's all right. You have to grow up sometime. But," he said, "you will be sure to stay within shouting distance. The wind can take a sudden turn, you know, and upset all your plans!"

"Yes, we promised," said Dai, who was feeling better by the moment.

Mama didn't insist on practice that evening, nor did she speak to Dai more than once about going to bed. He was ready.

Dai was up and doing early next morning. He remembered to borrow Papa's toolbox and as soon as Mama had given him breakfast and packed his lunch he was off. Grandma Craig and Papa hadn't even come downstairs when he left.

A sharp whistle brought Arky out of the house and Elmer was just coming around the corner. The morning was bright and sunny with a sea breeze and hardly a cloud in the sky. There was the usual flutter of gulls and water birds as they crossed the meadows, and the boys arrived at Cap Brockway's

M.deA.

just as he did. The day's business began and what a day it was.

Dai, who really liked working with tools, especially with wood, expected to have the mast stepped by the end of the day. Perhaps, even to have all the rigging done. But he found that there was much more to rigging a boat than he had thought.

"Will we be able to sail her tomorrow?" he asked Cap Brockway.

"*Tomorrow!* Huhnh! It's goin' to take a lot longer than one day to do what's needed on that old scow. First, you gotta get all the knots off that mast, so's the hoops'll slide easy. You gotta smooth the gaff and the boom, too, after you saw off the ends of the branches. Here, let me show you." Cap Brockway took up a small saw and set to work on the longest piece of spruce. "Now, I've got my own work to do. When you get all the branch ends sawed off, I'll show you how to use the draw shave. Is there one in that tool kit?" He helped Dai look through the tools, but didn't find a draw shave.

"Well, I think there's one I can lend you, but mind, be careful with it." He lifted one off the wall where other tools hung, and showed it to the boys, then hung it up again, speaking as he moved.

"Then you have to sandpaper and varnish her. It'll take a while. Now stay over on this side of the shop where you won't git in my way."

Dai set to work. It wasn't too difficult for him to saw through the spruce and when he was tired, Arky did pretty well, too, although he hadn't had much experience with tools. Elmer did his part by carrying branches to the trash heap, where they would be burned, and by chipping bark off the tree trunks.

Because Dai had discovered the boat, he considered himself to be the captain. Most of the time the boys accepted his commands, meekly, and did their best to be helpful. After lunch, which they ate outside near the water, Cap Brockway showed Dai how to use the plane and the draw shave, smoothing down the knots to the stem and the clean wood. It gave off a fragrant odor as they worked.

"Smells like Christmas," said Arky.

By late afternoon, Cap Brockway left his work and helped the boys step the mast. He fitted it into place with chips and pieces while the boys held it steady.

Then he said, "You younguns better git on home now. It's near suppertime. Come back tomorrow."

Dai put the tools back in place; the boys waved good-by and left.

They felt pleasantly tired as they trudged over the marshy ground toward home. They grinned at each other, feeling proud of the day's work.

"See you in the morning—early, seven o'clock!" Dai called to Elmer as he turned off to his street.

"Okay, theven!" said Elmer.

The boys met as planned, shivering slightly in the early morning.

All day, they worked on the other spars for gaff and boom, scraping, planing, sanding. It took still another day to varnish them, to add the other necessary things, such as cleats for halyards, and to sew the hoops on the sail, now mended and hemmed.

Dai was by now feeling quite important in his role as captain.

"How do you think that cleat is going to hold the halyard if you don't set it straight?" he yelled at Elmer.

"You'd better sew those hoops on stronger than that," he directed Arky as they sat together with needles and thread. "Look! I'm doing it three times as many as you do. Take three or four extra stitches to hold the end good." Arky nodded meekly and went back over what he had done.

"We haven't named her!" Dai suddenly remembered. "Let's call her *Kate* after my mother. After all, she made the sail, and if we didn't have a sail we wouldn't have a boat, right?"

"Right!" Arky and Elmer agreed.

"You can paint the name on tomorrow," Cap

Brockway said. "But now, you younguns, git for home. It's late." Then, seeing the boys' disappointment, he went on, "Well, might as well take you aboard and show you how to manage the sail. But, here, take this bailing can. You must *never, never* go out without a bailing can. Never! Any boat can spring a leak, especially this old tub."

He saw to the boys getting aboard, holding the boat steady, and as he stepped over the side, he reminded them to observe the rules of sailing. He had told them all of it before as they talked over lunch or while working, but now, they were under sail and what he said had more meaning for them.

"You hold the tiller so—easy, easy, but firm, mind you. And the sail must be trimmed to suit the breeze. You go about this way." He trimmed the sail so the boat turned in the other direction. "And you let out the sheet in a puff of wind so—and tack—like this," Cap Brockway took the boat around.

She sailed in the gentle breeze like the lady she was named for—*Kate*. After all, Dai told his mother, "You mended the sail."

CHAPTER 7

On their way home, a brindle bulldog rushed out of an alley as they passed. Dai stopped. Remembering Roy, he bent to fondle the dog's ears.

"I bet he's hungry, poor boy," he said, as the dog sniffed at his legs, wagging his stumpy tail. "I never saw this dog before. He doesn't belong around here. Let's see if he follows. C'mon, boy!" The boys ran, and the dog followed Dai, keeping close to his heels. Arky and Elmer left them at the corner, and went on, but the dog stayed with Dai all the way home until Mama met them at the door. Then the dog tore up the steps, then stopped, wagging his tail.

As always, Mama was sympathetic to a hungry animal, boy or dog. She set out scraps for him in the yard.

"Can I keep him?" begged Dai. "Can I?"

"We'll see what Papa says," Mama promised. "If we inquire about his owner and nobody claims him—perhaps. He seems gentle enough, but very excitable. He *rushes* so! I thought he was going to knock me over. At first, you think he is really fierce! Yet, when you touch him, he's gentle as a baby. Those teeth on his under jaw don't mean a thing, do they!" Mama touched the dog's head. "The hair looks stiff, yet it's really silky."

The dog made noises in his throat as if answering her and wagged and wagged his whole hind end.

"I'll call him Brin. That's it," Dai said, just as if he already owned him. "He's brindle color. Brin is just right. C'mon, boy."

Brin seemed to fill a need left by Roy's death. Papa was right, Dai thought, I can love another dog.

When Papa came home and found the dog there, he was doubtful about letting Dai keep him.

"We'll put a piece in the paper," he said, "and I'll inquire around to see if anyone claims him. If not, then I guess he can stay. He's very impulsive," Papa added, as Brin went into action when a cat came out of a neighbor's house. But Brin had already lost interest when the cat settled down under a tree.

No one claimed the dog, so Brin became a member of the household. He followed Dai everywhere and became a partner in the boys' activities. He went with them to Cap Brockway's boat yard and shared the adventures aboard the *Kate*. He accompanied them to the beach and enjoyed setting forth in a burst of speed after every living thing that took his sudden fancy. Nothing stopped him except his own loss of interest.

Once, he barely missed the wheels of a trolley car when he chased a cat. Another day, when a ball rolled across the pavement, he suddenly took off after it and all but upset an elderly gentleman, who became very angry, shaking his fist at Brin, then at the boys. "You young scamps, look out where you're going!"

Brin annoyed the next-door neighbor by flying through her garden after a cat and muddying the sheets hanging to dry. "That crazy animal! He ought to be tied up," she shouted.

But his ugly face was so lovable when he was quiet that everybody forgave him, even the neighbor, especially when Dai said, "I'm sorry. I will tie him up!" Mama gave Dai a length of clothesline and Papa bought a long lead to give Brin the run of the yard. He seemed to sense that he must be still while in the boat and while Dai painted the name *Kate* on the bow.

Cap Brockway again cautioned the boys about care in sailing. "Look out for that bulldog. He's pretty rambunctious. Still, he can swim and might be a help in case of need. *Watch* him though! And watch the tide!"

All went well for a while. It was hot and humid with an offshore breeze, then it changed to bright, clear weather with a gentle wind off the sea, perfect sailing weather.

"Mama, can't I cut out practicing for a while? Please," Dai begged, and Mama agreed to let him take a week off except for fifteen minutes a day, "just to keep your hand in," she said.

Papa warned him, "Do as Cap says. Keep out of the current that might sweep you out to sea, and stay within shouting distance in case of trouble!"

There were a few arguments and a few incidents. In a sudden jibe, Arky was smacked on the head by the boom and the tiller snapped off when Elmer tried to hold it steady. Fortunately, they were not far from the dock, so they could lower the sail and row in. Next day, they mended the tiller.

"Might as well do our own fixing," Dai said, importantly. "We'll just stow the toolbox under the stern sheets for now."

On another day, all seemed smooth sailing. The boys were in a sort of dream with the delicious reality of being in their very own craft.

"A-a-h—" sighed Dai, as he held the sheet gently in his hand. "The sky is blue, the breeze is just right, the sun not too hot. It's heaven!"

"What could be better than this?" agreed Arky, holding the tiller.

"It-th thwell!" declared Elmer, lounging on the deck.

They were conquerors. They were kings!

Suddenly, there was a bump. Brin scrambled to his feet.

"I thee land!" cried Elmer. "We're aground!" His eyes popped.

Dai tightened his hold on the sheet.

Arky felt the tiller jerked from his hand.

And there was land, land to the right of them, land to the left of them, land!

They were not aground. They were ashore!

All hands got out, shoved and pushed till water lapped at the gunnels, then Elmer and Dai, back aboard shoving with the oars, and Arky still pushing, got her afloat.

A few days later, the boys had just raised the sail and loosed the painter when Dai discovered the oars had been stolen. He rounded on Arky and Elmer as if he suspected them of treachery, but it was only shock that made it seem so.

"Who stole those oars?" he bellowed.

Both boys looked angry and hurt. They loved the old wreck as much as he did, and showed their resentment. Dai calmed down.

"Now what will we do?" he sank onto the deck, forgetting that the boat was untied. A sudden puff of wind sent them out into the channel and all hands were kept busy.

Dai grabbed the sheet and shouted to Arky, "GO ABOUT! GO ABOUT! Hard a lee." And to Elmer—

"Look out for the boom and hold on. We're going about!"

They narrowly missed a sneak box just coming out of the cove. As they rounded it safely, a rowboat appeared with two big boys at the oars. Oars that looked suspiciously like those Cap Brockway had given them. The rowboat went out into the channel as fast as the big boys could pull it. Surely, they were the oars belonging to the *Kate*. They had the same streaky green paint on the blades, the same worn edges.

"Look! *There* they go, the thieves!" Arky let go the tiller for a moment and jumped up, pointing to the big boys who were drawing away as fast as they could.

Dai ran to the side, Elmer got up to look, too, but lost his balance. Brin slid across the deck and— PLOP! over they all went into deep water with the *Kate* lying on her side and Elmer out of sight.

Frantically, Dai dived under the boat looking for him. The lines and sail hampered him. He saw Arky and Brin swim to the surface, but where was Elmer?

Holding his breath, Dai pushed aside the curtain of sail and there was Elmer, his face green and froglike through the water. He was gasping and struggling to free himself when Dai grasped him by the hair and, treading water, got him out from under the sail.

Brin was swimming about, crazy with excitement but not much help.

Dai's shouts brought Cap Brockway from his work and he came running to the dock, but when he saw all three boys safe, he let them handle the situation.

With great effort, Dai boosted Elmer up onto the centerboard, where he could hold on.

"Hold on for dear life, *and don't let go!* When we get her upright, you'll go under for a minute, but hang onto the gunnel and we'll soon haul you aboard." Arky, meanwhile, had clambered up, standing ready to lend his weight while Dai swam around to lift the mast from the water.

When the halyards were free, the gaff and hoops holding the sail to the mast were pushed back to

the deck, so that it was not too hard to get the mast free of the water and gradually right the boat. She was badly waterlogged, but she came upright. Elmer held on as he'd been told. Treading water, Arky bailed furiously with his hands and Dai with the can, rescued when it floated near. Brin, swimming about, finally made it to land.

Suddenly, Dai noticed they were drifting, not toward land, but seaward. He heard Cap Brockway screaming at them. "The tide is going out!"

"Hey! We'll go out to sea! Arky, quick!" Both boys swimming, with Elmer guiding, struggled to get the boat, heavy with water and very unsteady, into shallow water at the marsh's edge. Dai caught the bucket thrown by Cap Brockway. They finished bailing her out, then dragged her to the dock.

Cap Brockway stood watching, one hand on his hip.

"What happened? You might have been drowned, you know." He looked very serious.

Dai poured out the story of the stolen oars, the boys he had seen with them, the near collision with the sneak box, and—"Oh! My father's toolbox! I forgot about that. Oh! It must be at the bottom of the Thoroughfare! Oh!"

"Well, it's no joke to lose your father's toolbox. Why didn't you leave it with me?"

He still looked serious, but when he beheld the three bedraggled sailors and the panting Brin, he began to laugh. But he was a kind man and soon had them inside the shop where the boys took off their wet clothes and spread them out to dry.

"Now let's see," he said. "I got no oars to spare and don't know when I will. Suppose you boys just forget the sailboat for a while. I think I shouldn't have let you use that old wreck anyway. You might 'a drowned. You managed, but another year on your age won't hurt none." Meantime, he was getting out his lunch box and passing out sandwiches, opening a jug of milk for each boy to take a turn. The food was comforting, but Dai was wondering what Papa would say when he learned about the lost toolbox.

"*Now,* I'll get it," he sighed. "My father will be pretty mad about the tools."

"Will he lick you?" Arky wanted to know.

"I'd rather he would than to give me the lecture I'll get."

Elmer just sat and mumbled into his sandwich and sniffed.

"What do you think *I'll* get? My mother doethn't even know I go out in the boat! She won't let me ever come over here again." He looked so mournful, Cap Brockway reached out and patted his head.

"Never mind, there are lots of other things to do. You better learn to swim."

"Well," Dai said, getting up to put on his clothes, "we might as well get home and face it. C'mon, Brin, let's go." They thanked Cap Brockway for his help and went their way, each to his own house. Elmer was still sniffing from being so long under water. Dai wondered what Elmer's mother would do to him. He wondered all the way home what his own mother would say when she saw his damp clothes. He went in by the front door, hoping he could get upstairs without being seen. Sometimes Mama fainted when things upset her too much. Would she now?

She did.

CHAPTER 8

Mama recovered rather quickly. Grandma chafed her hands and gave her some water, and asked Dai what had happened and how he came to be so drowned-looking.

"Drowned?" Mama wailed, "I knew it, I knew it—" and almost went off again, but Grandma soothed her as always saying, "It's all right, it's all right," and soon Mama was sitting up.

Then Papa came in.

The minute he saw how pale and shaken Mama still looked and Dai's guilty face, he frowned.

"*What*'s the trouble? What *have you done* now?" He turned to Dai, who wondered how Papa could always tell when something was wrong.

"The sailboat upset," Dai began, then stopped.

"Was anybody with you except Arky and Brin? *Tell me!*" he thundered.

"Yes, Elmer. He got caught under the sail—and—"

"WELL, out with it, what else? Is he all right? Was anybody else with you?"

"No—but—"

"Come, come! Tell me, what else?"

"I borrowed your tools to fix the tiller—and—"

"And—they are all at the bottom of the channel, I suppose. *Is that it?*" Papa's voice grew louder and more and more threatening; then as Dai nodded, Papa sighed resignedly.

"*What* are you going to do next? You know how you upset your mother. I guess we must just be thankful you or anyone else is not at the bottom of the channel, too. Too bad about the tools. I was going to build a house for Brin in the yard, and perhaps I'll have to return the surprise I brought home."

The way Papa looked at him, pursing his mouth, nodding his head up and down, was worse for Dai than if his father had taken off his shoe and paddled him with it.

What was the surprise? He didn't dare ask. Papa just stood there for a moment, then said, "Come and see."

What could it be?

Dai followed Papa to the kitchen door. Grandma and Mama came too. There, tethered to the apple tree, was a billy goat complete with horns and whiskers.

Brin was there, too, and the way those two animals behaved toward each other was so funny that Papa, Mama, and Grandma laughed. Dai, relieved that all was well again, laughed, too, first at Billy, who pranced on his little cloven hoofs, bleating, his ears pricked forward. Then at Brin, who minced up to Billy, his ugly jaw thrust forward, uttering threats. Then they all laughed at each other. They laughed till the tears ran down.

The two animals advanced and retreated for a while, till Billy backed into one corner of the yard and Brin into another, and there they sat it out.

"Is he for keeps?" asked Dai, when the laughter had quieted.

"Yes, one of the men in the company owed me some money, so we traded for the goat. Now he's yours. Perhaps if you have him to care for you will stay away from that treacherous old boat and the Thoroughfare."

"Oh, I will, I will." Dai ran to throw his arms around Billy's neck. "Ba-a-a-," said Billy.

Dai was already thinking of a way to hitch Billy to the cart. How handy it would be to ride behind Billy when Mama sent him on an errand to buy eggs, or to the dock where the fishermen came in from the sea with weakfish and sea bass. Sometimes they brought in great tuna weighing hundreds of pounds, or squid with long tentacles. Dai liked to go to the docks. Often, fishermen sat mending their nets and if one listened, he could hear tales of the sea.

Dai decided to consult Frank.

"Frank, can you help me find a way to hitch up this Billy goat I've got?"

"Sure," said Frank. "Let's look around and see what we can find." He led Dai to the back of the workshop where a heap of things lay against the fence. There were pieces of old harness, lengths of strap, and two buckles, the remains of a lady's carriage. Most of it had been used to repair other vehicles, but the thills (shafts) were there and the

91

whiffletree and swivel. These were just what was
needed. The thills were too long, of course, and
somewhat heavy for a cart, so Frank shaved them
down, leaving some wide enough to attach to the

whiffletree. That had to be shortened, too. Frank whistled as he worked, as if he enjoyed what he was doing. He answered Dai's questions and showed him how to put the harness together.

It had begun to rain, so no one came in for repairs and nobody came into the livery stable to hire a horse or pony. Frank found a small buckle to fasten the halter and with a big needle punched several eyelets so it would fit.

In an hour or so, it was finished. Dai thanked Frank and dragged the cart home in the rain.

Billy and Brin had made friends and stood together under the apple tree.

The tree was dripping and both animals looked forlorn. I must build a house for Brin and one for Billy, Dai thought. Perhaps Papa will help. He would search for boards washed up on the beach.

Next day, when the rain had stopped, Elmer and Arky came to see Billy, and they laughed, too, at the funny animal.

The boys held Billy while Dai hitched him to the cart and off they went, down to the boardwalk—Dai riding, Brin running with the boys. "Now that you won't be sailing any more, it's time to begin your practice," Mama called from the front door. "You know it's getting late in the season and you must be ready to begin lessons again. Don't forget!"

"I won't," Dai called back, then muttered to himself, "If I hafta, I hafta, I suppose."

Billy was fun for a few days. The boys took turns riding in the cart. There was room for only one to ride and one was enough for Billy to pull. More and more often, Arky found something else to do, and Elmer said he would rather play ball.

Billy hadn't been with the family very long before he got Dai into trouble. One Monday, Dai forgot to tie him up. Billy wandered into the next yard where freshly laundered clothes hung to dry and chewed up enough of a white dress so it could never be worn again.

While Mama was serving supper, there was a loud knock at the kitchen door. There stood Mr. Jameson, looking very fierce. Behind him was Mrs. Jameson, weeping. Mr. Jameson had the goat by the collar. Dai wondered why he sounded so angry.

"Mrs. Murphy," he said in a loud voice, "you'll have to keep these animals of yours tied up better or I'm going to the police! Your dog muddied the sheets last week chasing a cat and now, this creature has chewed up my wife's best white dress so it can never be worn again. I don't like to make trouble, but enough's enough!"

"I didn't want to say anything on account of being friends," said Mrs. Jameson tearfully, "but it *is* my best dress." She dabbed at her eyes with her handkerchief.

Mama asked them to come in and have coffee. Dai slipped away into the front room.

"I can't tell you how sorry I am," Dai heard Mama say as she poured the coffee.

"We will do the best we can to make up for the loss of your dress and John will take care of this situation right away. To tell the truth, I've had enough of it myself."

Did Mama mean to get rid of Billy? Well—Dai thought, then I wouldn't have to build him a house nor take him to the fields to eat. I'll have more time to play with Arky. I'll still have Brin.

When Papa came home, Mama told him about Mrs. Jameson's dress and how embarrassed she had been. Papa said, "I guess I shouldn't have taken him. I didn't realize how much trouble he could be."

"Well," said Mama, "I tried to put up with him, but as Mr. Jameson said, 'enough's enough!' I just can't stand him around any longer and having to remind Dai to feed him and tie him up."

"Yes," Papa nodded. "I can see he's too much trouble."

Papa found a farmer living near Pleasantville who kept goats to provide goats' milk for the hospital. He took Dai with him to keep Billy quiet in the back of a delivery wagon Papa borrowed. When Dai saw all the little kids with their mothers frolicking in the meadow, standing on their hind legs, prancing about, he felt sad at giving up Billy and wished they could take one of the kids home with them, but Papa said, "NO *SIR!* As your mother said, 'enough's enough.'"

CHAPTER 9

Summer was nearing its end.

"The Steel Pier will close in a week or two," Papa said. "We are getting ready to take the company on tour for a few weeks, going as far west as Cincinnati and Chicago, perhaps."

Arky said his father would soon be through playing at the hotel and they would go back to Philadelphia any day now. Elmer was visiting his grandmother in Baltimore.

The ponies were back in the livery stable where Frank would care for them through the winter. The rolling chairs had been put away and many of the stores had closed. The city seemed deserted.

To be sure, the swimming was delicious in the warm water of late summer but Dai felt suddenly lonely. Papa had been so busy engaging people to perform each week and getting ready for the tour, he hadn't had time for anything else. Dai wandered listlessly into the parlor wishing that Papa could have taken him to the meadows to shoot ducks. He lifted the gun from its corner, hefted it, ran his fingers over the smooth wooden parts and the shining metal. Wouldn't Mama be pleased if he brought home a duck for dinner? He shifted the gun to balance in his hand, went to the secretary and took out the box of bird shot. Of course he had promised Papa not to fool with it, but he couldn't wait forever for Papa to go with him. Brin, sensing excitement, snuffled and grunted.

"Ssssh!" Dai cautioned him. I'll see if Arky has gone home, he thought. Elmer's too young for this expedition, even if he was still here.

Dai slipped quietly out the front way and down the street to find Arky, who came running out at Dai's whistle. "What's up?" he called, buttoning his shirt. His eyes bulged as he spied the shotgun. "The *shot*gun?"

"How about goin' to the meadows to shoot duck? Look!"

Arky ran back, opened the door, and shouted to his mother, "We're going to the meadows!" He slammed the door and ran to catch up with Dai before his mother had time to object. She did come to the door, but the boys were rounding the corner.

The boys hurried out of sight. When they got to the meadows Brin rushed here and there and water birds flew up in alarm as their territory was invaded. There were white egrets, marsh hens, swooping terns with rosy bills, and ducks of every kind.

Dai loaded the gun with bird shot. Where should he aim?

A mallard rose from the marsh. Dai raised the gun to his shoulder.

He fired—but missed the moving target.

Frustrated, frightened, and angry, he slammed the butt of the gun down on the turf.

Bang!

The second barrel went off.

The shot went straight through the brim of Dai's hat, sending it flying and just grazing his forehead with the heat of it.

Dai's eyes popped. Terrified, he sat down suddenly, his face white, his hand covering his mouth as if to keep from screaming. Brin rushed up to comfort him.

Arky didn't say a word, but looked as if he had seen a ghost.

When he could speak, Dai said, very quietly, "Let's go home!"

Arky nodded.

Dai picked up the gun very cautiously and the two frightened boys went slowly home. And that was that. They parted without a word.

"Is that you, Dailey?" Mama called from upstairs. Dai had come in as quietly as he knew how, but Brin's toenails clicked on the floor.

"Yea, it's me. I'm hungry." He gingerly opened the door of the secretary to put back the box of shot.

"You always are," said Mama, as she started downstairs.

Dai sighed with relief. Never again would he touch that gun without Papa's permission and help. He remembered the holes in his hat and pulled it off just as Mama came into the room.

"You look a mite peaked," she said, smoothing his head; then, seeing Dai's guilty look, asked "WHAT HAVE YOU BEEN UP TO?" and noticed the gun standing at a different angle. She sensed that it had been used and fell to the floor in a faint.

Dai, almost too frightened to move, knelt beside her, then screamed for Grandma Craig.

She came running down the steps.

"There, there," she soothed as she touched Mama's hand, and sent Dai to the kitchen for water and a cloth, dipping it into the cool water and laying it on Mama's forehead.

"What happened?" Grandma questioned Dai.

Before he could answer, Mama's eyes opened slowly. She sat up, looking bewildered. Then, "Oh, yes, yes—I remember. Oh!" She closed her eyes again for a moment.

She needed only to look at Dai to be sure that he would not touch the gun again. She didn't question him, only picked up the hat and examined the holes. Grandma, too, kept silent. Dai just shook his head from side to side.

When she could speak, Mama said, "You know, of course, how Papa will feel about this. You promised him, remember? You *promised* not to touch that gun until he gave you permission when he was with you."

Yes, Dai knew. How he dreaded what Papa would say!

"You will stay in the house this afternoon and you will practice two hours, beginning right after lunch."

Dai nodded. He was still too frightened to talk. He had been scared out of his wits.

After the long practice, the afternoon dragged endlessly. When Papa came home, it happened that Mama met him in the hall. As he greeted her, he held her off to look at her.

"You look pale, Kate," he said. "What's the matter?" He frowned in concern.

"Oh, I'm a little tired," she said. "Come, let's have dinner. Then, I think Dai wants to talk to you. But let's eat first."

But it was not in Papa's nature to put things off, especially if, as he suspected, it was a matter of discipline.

"What has he done *now?* Dai*ley?* Where are you? Come here!" Papa went into the parlor where Dai was. He had been trying to read, but all he could think about was how he had nearly been killed and wonder what Papa would say to him for breaking his promise.

"Lift your head and look at me. What HAVE YOU DONE! Speak!"

"The shotgun, I—I—I fired it and it went off through my hat." He picked up the hat from the chair where Mama had dropped it and showed Papa the holes in the brim.

"WHAT!!! After all I said to you and you promised? How can I trust you again? Do you realize you might have been killed if the shot had been an eighth of an inch closer to your head?"

Dai seemed to have no words, but he said, "Yes, sir," very low.

Suddenly, Papa sat down. Dai saw the color leave his face. He was almost as white as Mama had been when she fainted. Then he said, very gently, "Son, I hope you realize how serious this is. I'm quite sure you wouldn't take the gun again, but I shall remove temptation. We'll give the gun to Vic Richards. He lost his and will be glad to have it." Papa paused, took out his handkerchief, and blew his nose.

Then he took Dai's hand in his, looked into his

eyes, and said, "It pays to keep promises, my boy. Come, Mama's waiting and Grandma has dinner on the table." He rose, put his arm around Dai, and walked him in to the dining room.

While they were eating, Papa said, "I've been thinking, Kate. This gun business has upset me a great deal and I think it has upset you even more. You worry me. I think you need a rest. Besides, I realized this summer I think that Dailey should go to the Coombes Conservatory in Philadelphia where he will have a more complete musical education. Mr. Bucholz is retiring as you know, so that is all right. It is too far for Dailey to go back and forth to Philadelphia for his lessons, so I will write to Aunt Emily to ask if he can live with her for the winter. He can go to the Christian Brothers School a few blocks away and to the Conservatory. I know she will be glad of your company, Dai, now that Uncle Jim is gone, but I hope you will be thoughtful of her and not give any trouble, will you?"

Dai nodded. He wondered what it would be like living in downtown Philadelphia. It would be different from West Philadelphia and all the boys would be new. He thought about Ted and Butch and the others. They would be starting school again, too, at Heston. Miss Winnemore would be their teacher now. She had always seemed so pleasant.

Dai was quiet so long, Papa said, "Well, don't you like the idea?"

"Oh, yes, of course." But he looked ruefully at

Mama and Grandma Craig. "I guess it would be all right, if I can take Brin. Can I, Papa? I wouldn't want to leave him, too."

"I think so. I think Aunt Em won't mind if you take good care of him, keep him quiet and out of mischief. You must keep him clean and see that he is fed. You know Aunt Em is very particular. And you must promise to do your practicing faithfully. I hope you are old enough now to know what a promise means."

"Yes, I know. I'll take good care of Brin and I will practice. *I promise.*" Dai looked at Papa when he said, "I promise."

"Good. I'll write to Aunt Emily tonight, so we should hear from her soon. We are about ready to go on tour but you can manage, I'm sure. It will be quiet here now that vacations are over."

"The house will seem very empty with both Dai and you away," said Mama.

"Who will eat my oatmeal cookies?" asked Grandma a little sadly.

CHAPTER 10

Within a few days Papa had gone to New York, where he was to meet the other members of the troupe. Before he left, an article appeared in the local newspaper. Mama and Grandma were reading it when Dai came in. It began: "I have received word that John E. Murphy and his Minstrel Band, who have been entertaining vast assemblages on the Steel Pier in Atlantic City since the very early summer, closed their season last night in a blaze of glory. The audience was truly representative—"

"Aren't you proud of Papa?" Mama asked. "Isn't this splendid publicity?"

Dai read the clipping Grandma had just cut from the paper. "Boy!" he burst out. "Isn't that something? Wow! Wait till I show Arky!" Then he realized Arky had gone home. Would he see him again?

The letter had come from Aunt Em, saying how happy she would be to have Dai to stay with her. She said Dai might bring the dog if he would look after him and that she had made arrangements for Dai to attend the Brothers' school and the Conservatory.

It was rather exciting to think of living in the

center of the city with Aunt Em, to be going to a new school and to the Conservatory, but Dai wondered if he would be homesick. Aunt Em was nice but she wasn't Mama. And Grandma Craig wouldn't be there to comfort him when he was hurt, to coax him with the things she baked. Would Aunt Em have homemade bread?

Mama and Grandma bustled about, getting Dai's clothes ready, mending his stockings, a tear in his knickers, ironing his shirts and round collars, laying out his best shoes and black silk ties.

Then it was time to go.

Dai said good-by to Grandma Craig and Mama took him to the train. She made little jokes on the way as they rode in the trolley. Brin snuffled and grunted, but finally settled down. Dai was very quiet.

"Now," said Mama, "I won't have to hang up your clothes, nor get your meals, nor scold you for bringing in mud on your feet, nor keep after your practicing." She laughed shakily, but her eyes were full of tears. "I won't have anything to do."

Dai just swallowed. He was too big to cry, at eleven going on twelve.

"Cheer up!" Mama kissed him. "Your face is as long as a wet week!"

Dai grinned, but his eyes were not smiling. He lifted Brin up the train steps and found a seat where there was room for him. Then Dai waved out of the window to Mama as the train pulled out. He couldn't reach the luggage rack so he stowed his bags on the floor near his feet.

It was exciting to be on the train again, but sad to be leaving Mama and Grandma, knowing Papa was away for a long time and that summer was gone.

What would it be like to live at Aunt Em's? Would the Brothers' school be like Heston school? Would they have a baseball team? What would the Conservatory be like? Would he have to practice more than ever?

Dai held tight to Brin's leash till he went to sleep.

He felt very much alone. He stared out at the meadows, remembering the happy days with Arky and Elmer, the frightening spill into the Thoroughfare, the terrifying accident with the shotgun, the lazy days when all was well.

Before he knew it the train was in Camden.

Dai felt in his pocket to make sure he still had money for the ferry to Philadelphia and the trolley. He felt quite grown-up. He stood at the rail on the ferryboat, wondering at the city, looming up before him across the Delaware River, with its church spires and the tower of City Hall. Somehow it seemed bigger than he'd remembered.

Mama had told him to take the trolley on Market Street and ask for a transfer down Tenth. It was too far to walk with his valise, violin case, and Brin's leash to hold, but was only about ten minutes by trolley. Dai was a little anxious for fear he would take the wrong car, and the conductor promised to let him know when they reached Reed Street.

Aunt Em was all ready for him with cake and

milk set out. She accepted Brin with good grace even though he pulled the leash out of Dai's hand and rushed through the entrance hall almost sweeping Aunt Em off her feet. When he had decided that it was safe for everybody, he settled down.

"We shall have to make a place for him in the yard, and when it gets cold he can have a blanket to sleep on. That way, he won't tear up the whole house."

She looked rather anxious. "There are some of Uncle Jim's boards left down in the cellar in his workshop. You can make him a little house, Dai."

"Yes, ma'am." Dai was delighted. It almost made him feel at home.

"Tomorrow, in the afternoon, you are to see Mr. Schradiech and arrange for your lessons. The Brothers' school is on Lombard Street and the Conservatory on Broad Street about five squares south. Now, let's take your things up to your room. You can leave your violin on the piano in the parlor." Aunt Em went ahead to the little room near the top of the stairs where Dai had slept before at Christmas time.

As she was leaving the room, Aunt Em said, "I've made arrangements for us to attend a concert tomorrow evening. A small group of musicians is giving a series of concerts at Musical Fund Hall. They are young people just beginning their careers, but they are professional. I think you will enjoy it."

"Oh, thank you. Yes, I will, I know I will." Dai

unpacked his bag and left his Sunday suit hanging where it would be handy. Perhaps it was going to be fun living in Philadelphia again. He thought about the old house in West Philadelphia and Butch and Ted. Would he ever see them?

Dai was startled out of sleep next morning by the rattle of iron-rimmed wheels on cobblestones. He blinked his eyes, wondering for a moment where he was. Instead of the flowered wallpaper he had been used to seeing when he woke, he found himself staring at a maplike pattern on the ceiling where rain had seeped in. Then he remembered. This was Aunt Em's house in Philadelphia, not home in Atlantic City. Instead of sea gulls wheeling in the sky, he could see roof tops and brick buildings. Instead of the roar of the surf, he heard the loud clatter of the city. He jumped out of bed and ran to the window. He could see over the high board fence and across Ninth Street into the stable yard of the bakery. The last wagon was just leaving the gate and a man was washing down the cobbles with a great hose. Then he heard a clamor at the front of the house. He ran out and down the hall to the front window. Wagons and carts were going in both directions and over the tops of them Dai could see the gray stone pile of Moyamensing prison. He shivered at the thought of anyone being shut up there away from everybody one cared for.

He could now hear other sounds of day's beginning, the iron clang of the stove lids lifted and set back. That meant breakfast was almost ready.

He washed hastily at the basin, dressed, slicked

his hair with the comb, and hurried downstairs, thinking of Brin and wondering if he had bothered Aunt Em. He was all the way down before he remembered that he had been told to use the back stairs.

"Hello!" she said, "here's our boy. What would you like for breakfast?"

"Anything, I guess," but Dai hoped it would be oatmeal cooked as Mama cooked it. He opened the back door and there was a scramble of feet on the linoleum as Brin rushed into the house. "Oh-o-o!" Aunt Em nearly upset the coffee she was carrying. Dai quieted Brin and he obediently lay down under the table ready for any bits of food Dai offered.

In spite of the near-by bakery, Aunt Em baked her own bread and made her own strawberry jam, a delicious finish for the oatmeal breakfast.

"The first thing we must do," said Aunt Em as they sat at table, "is to go to Wanamaker's and have you fitted for a uniform. All the boys at the Brothers' school are required to wear blue knickers, a jacket with military collar, and a plain white shirt. They may have one to fit you already made. We'll see. School begins next Tuesday, after Labor Day, so we haven't much time."

They set out after breakfast, going up Thirteenth Street. A trolley clanged to warn a wagon out of the way. Twice, they had to step around women scrubbing the marble steps in front of each house.

Dai had been in the big store before, but not often. They passed through the wide court and up in the elevators to the fourth floor where Dai found a uniform already made. It happened that a boy of his size had ordered it, then had moved away.

"Wasn't I lucky! Now I won't have to come here to be measured and fitted."

"The luck of the de Angeli's," agreed Aunt Em.

"This afternoon we will meet Mr. Schradiech and arrange for your violin lessons."

The Conservatory was south on Broad Street, several blocks from Aunt Em's.

Mr. Schradiech was a tall, fine-looking man.

"Well, son," he said to Dai, "are you ready for real work? Here, we *work*." He laughed as he spoke and added, "We have a good time, too. I know about where you are after studying with Bucholz, so first, let me take you to meet the teachers in the other classes. You must study harmony and the history of music if you are to be a true musician. Then next Tuesday, bring your fiddle and we'll see about your lessons."

Dai wondered if he could learn it all.

That evening the concert was delightful. Dai especially watched the violin player, a young man whose strong sensitive hands seemed to have magic in them. He thought about Peter Androssi, who had the same intense look.

That night, he dreamed about Peter. He dreamed that Peter was going through all the motions of playing, but there was no fiddle! No bow! He woke up laughing and thinking that maybe if he tried he could play as well as Peter.

On Tuesday Aunt Em took him to the school and introduced him to the brother in charge, Brother

Robert. As they neared the school, there had been some curious glances at the new boy. But there was so much teasing, punching, pulling, screaming, and tussling, the boys scarcely noticed Dai. Besides, Aunt Em was with him.

Dai was entered in the sixth grade. As the bell rang, the boys came into the room and settled down quietly.

Brother Robert said, simply, "Boys, this is Dailey de Angeli."

Through the morning, as the boys were called upon to recite, Dai learned their names. Tim Fogarty, Kevin Rafferty, Michael Shane, Ben Walton, Dan McGlone, and others.

The lessons weren't especially hard. The brothers were kind, but firm. They kept perfect order. No one was allowed even to whisper during class.

At recess time, and as soon as the boys were in the schoolyard, bedlam broke loose. Several of them gathered around Dai and began to tease him. One, Mike, he thought, who was taller than the others, jerked at his hair where a curl had turned up.

"Look at the mama's boy!"

"De Angeli!" cried another, "de Angeli! That's a wop's name." They all laughed and mocked him, grabbing at his clean white collar, yanking his jacket till a button flew off.

Dai was angry and a little frightened and didn't know quite what to do, so he didn't do anything, just stood and looked at the jeering crowd with a slight frown, his mouth a tight line.

Suddenly, there was Brother Robert in the midst of them. All he said, was, "BOYS!" and the boys melted away as if they had never heard of a boy called Dailey de Angeli.

The bell rang. Recess was over.

On the way to Aunt Emily's for lunch, only two or three of the boys jeered at him and they were careful to wait till they were out of hearing of the school.

"Wop, yourself!" he called back. He'd heard "wop" at Heston school and knew that it meant only that he was of Italian background. So? What difference did it make? Everybody came from *some*where. Dai thought of Great-grandfather Benedict and grinned.

He could hardly wait to see Brin, who went crazy with joy when Dai came into the alley.

I must make that house for him before the weather gets cold, he thought, and asked Aunt Em if he could go down in the cellar to look for wood to make it.

"Wait till Saturday," she said. "Then you can have the whole morning to do what you like." She sat down beside Dai while he ate the lunch cake she had put out for him. "Well, how did it go?"

"Oh, the kids teased me a lot. They jerked my jacket and pulled a button off. See! And they called me a wop."

"What did you do? Did you fight? I don't want you fighting!"

"No, I didn't. I didn't know what to do, so I just stood there. I guess it just wasn't any fun when

I didn't fight back. And then Brother Robert came out and that was it. I don't know about this afternoon though. Aunt Em, do I have to take my violin to school?"

"Well, you'd better. You will be taking it often and today you are to see Mr. Schradiech and arrange for your lesson time. You'd better practice a little before you go back to school so you will play well for Mr. Schradiech. Meanwhile I'll sew the button on your coat."

After his practice, Aunt Em smoothed Dai's hair, and sent him off again, carrying his violin case.

He wondered if there would be any trouble and wished Brin were with him. Brin's ferocious looks would ward off any attack. But Brin must stay home in the areaway and the small back yard.

Dai was rather short for eleven, but stocky and strong. He hadn't had much occasion to fight and wasn't anxious to meet again the big bully who had started trouble in the morning.

He had gone only a block or two when he passed an alley.

Two boys came running out yelling, "Sissie! Sissie!"

Two or three more came at him from the other side of the street. Suddenly, Dai was surrounded by boys, all yelling at the top of their voices, "SISSIE!" "MAMA'S BOY!!"

They yanked his jacket, some threw stones. This was too much. Dai laid about him with the fiddle box.

Wham! Bang! Whack! Heads went from one side to the other.

Just as suddenly there were no more boys near him. They had all fled, still screaming, still running, but on their way to school.

Dai stood alone and unhurt. Not a single boy was left.

He put down his fiddle box, buttoned his jacket, and went on his way, taking his time and feeling like a prince.

That was the end of his torment. He had stood his ground.

CHAPTER 11

After that first day at school when Dai had shown
his ability to defend himself, he was accepted as
one of the boys. He was almost as good at baseball
as Tim Fogarty, who lived not far from Aunt Em's,
and he could run as fast as Ben Walton, who lived
just around the corner. They played shinny and
duck-on-davy in the street and sometimes baseball,
but once when Dai was at bat, a neighbor's window was broken and Aunt Em didn't like that. So
they played ball in a vacant lot down the street.
Brin was always a part of the fun, but sometimes
his dashing in and out was a nuisance.

Meantime, Dai had begun the lessons at the Conservatory. Mr. Schradiech was famous for his
teaching methods and had written the exercise book
used by the students at the Conservatory and by
other schools. At his suggestion, Dai had gone with
Aunt Em to buy the book. As they went into the
music store, there was Arky buying the same book!
The boys had not seen each other since they had
left Atlantic City. Their greeting was typical—a
gentle punch in the ribs.

"Hi! Dailey! What are you doing here?"

"You going to the Conservatory, too?" Dai answered, pointing to the exercise book.

"Sure! Isn't it great? When is your lesson?"

"Saturday afternoon at two. When's yours?"

"Saturday, two-thirty."

"Maybe we'll meet there, huh? I'm staying with my aunt Emily. Here she is. Aunt Emily, this is Arky." Arky made his best bow and Aunt Emily smiled and shook his hand. Then she said, "You must come to see us sometime."

Arky thanked her and said, "I will."

"By," called Dai. "Still live in the same place?"

"Sure," said Arky as he went out the door. "See you—Saturday."

"Saturday!" Dai felt happier now that he had seen Arky again. They had become fast friends over the summer.

Just as Dai and Aunt Em were leaving, Peter Androssi came in. He, too, was there to buy the exercise book Mr. Schradiech had composed. Dai clapped Peter on the shoulder.

"Hi! You going to the Conservatory, too?"

"Unhuh. Pop sent me to buy the book we're going to use."

"I hate exercises, don't you?" asked Dai.

"Sure. But I guess we have to have 'em, don't we?" Peter said. Dai followed Aunt Em, who had gone out. "See you!" he called. He was remembering the school concert. He hoped Peter had learned to cut his fingernails and to bring his own fiddle if ever they should happen to be together on a program.

Every afternoon when Dai came home from school Aunt Em always had a glass of milk and cookies or fresh bread. Then she insisted that Dai begin his practicing immediately. And almost every day he complained bitterly.

"There's never any time to play with the kids. Why do I always, *always* have to practice?"

"But you are growing up now," Aunt Em said. "You know you promised your father. You know how much it means to him. He wants you to play well enough to earn your living as a violinist. And it is time for you to assume responsibility for yourself. If you learn this now, it will help you all your life."

In his heart, Dai knew Aunt Em was right but he didn't feel any happier. As the warm September days passed into weeks it seemed to him that the only fun he had was during the recess games and squabbles at school. The rest of his time was passed in a routine of errands for Aunt Em and runs with Brin, all too short to matter, and then lessons and PRACTICE. In spite of his good intentions, he felt as if he were being punished by having to give up so many hours to his violin. Much as he loved Great-grandfather's old fiddle, he sometimes wished it had been a baseball bat.

At least Aunt Em had taken him to two more concerts at Musical Fund Hall and once to the Academy of Music to hear Ysaye, a world-famous violinist. That had been a great treat.

Mr. Schradiech was now teaching Dai how to

play double stops and had given him an exercise of slurred notes to develop tone with the bow.

"It is the bow that gives tone and expresses feeling," he said. Taking the bow and fiddle from Dai, he played the exercise, his fingers flying over the strings while he drew the bow firmly but slowly over them. "This exercise requires one to play sixty notes on one bow. That is, playing all the notes while drawing the bow only once over the strings. So—

"Now, if you practice this as if all sixty notes must be played with only *half* the bow drawn, it will come easier. Always, it is best to do the most difficult thing *first,* then what follows seems easier. It is so with anything. Do the hard part first, then the rest is easy."

It sounded so easy when Mr. Schradiech said it, and when he had played the rippling notes. Dai went home to Aunt Em's determined to practice until he could do it as well.

But even while he practiced, he couldn't help hearing the boys in the street and wishing he could be with them. Yet, when he had finished the scales and studies, had spent a quarter hour on the special exercise, and turned to the composition book, he became enthralled by the melodies of Schubert, Bach, and Massenet. They carried him away, away from boys in the street, away from Aunt Em's parlor to a land of joy created by the fiddle and the bow.

Sometimes when he went for his lesson Mr.

Schradiech was pleased with his improvement but always he urged Dai to practice more.

"I am organizing a Youth Symphony," he said, "and would like you, Dailey, to be among the first violins. But I must be able to count on you, so work hard. You, I think, will have the first chair. Peter is extremely talented, but he is inclined to be careless."

"Peter Androssi? Yes. I know he is. He went to Heston school when I did. And I saw him that day when we both went to buy our exercise books. Arky was there, too."

"Well," Mr. Schradiech went on, "this will mean extra rehearsals, perhaps twice a week or more. If all goes well, we can give a concert at Thanksgiving time. Besides the extra rehearsals there would be your lesson, too. Are you willing?"

"Oh, yes, of course, Mr. Schradiech, thank you." But as he said it, Dai thought to himself, no time for playing ball, no shinny stick, no anything. Yet, he was flattered to have been chosen as one of the first violins, maybe even first chair. Papa would be pleased. Dai couldn't wait to write the good news.

One day, after school, as Dai was leaving, Brother Robert called him back and asked, "How are you doing with that violin you carry? Do you ever play for an evening's entertainment?"

"A few times, Brother Robert," Dai answered. "At school and at church socials. Why?"

"We are having a small celebration for one of

our young novices whose birthday it is. Would you come and play for us this evening? It is just here in our refectory and it wouldn't be late. Can you do it?"

"Yes, I'm sure it will be all right with my aunt Em. Could anyone accompany me?"

"I could, if the music is not too difficult. What would you play?"

"Oh, I could play Schubert's 'Serenade' or 'Traumerei.' What time?"

"From eight to nine or thereabout. It is kind of you. Thank you."

Most of the boys had gone on home when Dai left the school, but Tim had waited for him.

"Brother Robert asked me to play tonight for a novice's birthday. I said I would," Dai explained.

Aunt Em seemed pleased that Dai had been asked to play.

"But you will come straight home afterward, won't you. I don't like to have you on the streets after dark. You'd better go over those pieces, hadn't you?"

"UMHMMM! I will." That answered both questions.

The evening went well and the brothers were appreciative and sent Dai on his way feeling happy.

"Sometimes," he thought, "practice is worth it."

The next day at recess, as the boys streamed out into the playground, Ben Riley said, "Some people are teacher's pets! Yah!" pointing at Dai.

"Ye-ah, 'specially *violinists!*" Tim added laughing.

Dai was after him in seconds, grasping his arm, and kicking his knee to throw him, but Tim, ducking his head, made it a bony target for Dai's fist, which he meant to land in Tim's ribs. The knuckles cracked, sending pain up Dai's arm. He let go and Tim stumbled to right himself. Dai, nursing his injured hand, went off to a corner of the yard not saying a word. Jeers followed him. "Yah! Sissy!"

"Ya lost the fight, didn't ya?!" Tim stood aside, rubbing the back of his head.

When school was out, Dai went on his way alone. Tim, his best friend, passed him, but didn't speak—just went on with Ben. Suddenly, Dai remembered Ted and Butch, his old friends. I'm just not going home to Aunt Em's, he thought. I'm not going to rehearsal either, and today, I'm NOT going to PRACTICE! My hand hurts anyway. He turned at the next street, going north instead of to Aunt Em's. He was filled with anger, which carried him along till he came to Market Street, where he had to stop and think how to get to West Philadelphia. Then he remembered that Lancaster Avenue branched off from Market at about Thirty-fourth Street.

He wished he didn't have his fiddle and music case to carry, but never mind, he was on his way to see real friends. It was a long way, past Wanamaker's, and around City Hall, past Broad Street Station, the shops getting smaller, then giving way to houses. He crossed the bridge over the Schuylkill River, stopping to look down at a passing boat, then trudged on to Lancaster Avenue and his old neighborhood.

It took about an hour to reach Heston school, then another block or two and Dai was in the midst of the team. There was Ted, and Butch, and the others. For a moment they looked at him curiously. He had grown through the summer. Then there were smiles and yells—"Hi! Hi! Where've you been?" Ted poked him in the stomach, Butch grabbed his arm. It was a great welcome.

A boy came running out of the house where Dai had lived and Nerky said, "Hey! This is the boy who used to live in your house. This is Dai de Angeli."

"Hi!" They greeted each other.

For about an hour, it was fun to be one of the team again. Then Dai began to have the strangest feeling that he *must* go. Where? Home? No. Home was in Atlantic City now. He must go—go back to Aunt Em's. It was too late for rehearsal. It was almost suppertime and he had an hour's walk back downtown.

"Got to go!" he said, picking up his fiddle box and music case. "By!" He began to run.

Dai soon stopped running. He was beginning to be tired and anxious. Aunt Em would be wondering where he was. Perhaps she would be angry. Mr. Schradiech would wonder why he hadn't come to rehearsal. Would he scold? Would he give Peter first chair? He was so tired, but he kept walking as fast as he could, going down alleys and small streets in the direction of Aunt Em's, hoping they were short cuts.

Aunt Em met him at the door. As he feared, she was angry and frightened.

"WHERE HAVE YOU BEEN? I've been waiting supper for you for an hour! Where have you *been?*" By now Dai was exhausted and near to tears himself. He dropped his fiddle case and music bag and threw his arms around Aunt Em's waist. Her anger vanished as she put her arms around him.

"I was *so* worried," she said. "I just couldn't imagine where you could be after rehearsal time was up." She sniffed a little, then asked again, "Where *were* you?"

Then it all came out—how he'd had a fight with Tim, had remembered his old friends, and suddenly couldn't bear the thought of rehearsal or practicing.

"I just *went.* That's all. I just had to go out to West Philadelphia. Then, all of a sudden, I just *had* to come home again."

"Well, it's all over now. Come, eat your supper. I'm afraid it's not very hot." Aunt Em brought the food from the kitchen and sat down with Dai while he ate and told about his long walk and about the boy who lived in the old house.

When Dai went to rehearsal on Thursday, Mr. Schradiech was quite severe. "You remember, Dailey, I trusted you to be faithful at rehearsals. Where were you Tuesday?"

Dai had to repeat his story as he had told it to Aunt Em.

"Well, don't let it happen again. I notice you

have a little trouble with fingering. You must practice steadily you know."

"I will," Dai promised.

Next morning, as Dai left for school, Tim came around the corner and greeted him as if nothing had happened. "Hi!" he called, and crossed the street to join Dai, who was carrying his fiddle case.

"Gonna play ball this afternoon?"

"Can't," Dai lifted his fiddle case. Tim understood. Not a word was said about the fight. They were friends again.

For a while after Mr. Schradiech's serious talk with him Dai practiced regularly. His hand hurt in certain positions and interfered somewhat with his fingering but he tried not to show that it bothered him at rehearsals. And every day after he had soaked his hand in hot water following Aunt Em's instructions his fingers were less painful.

It seemed a long, long time since he had left Mama at the station in Atlantic City. Letters came from her every week. Sometimes, Papa wrote. His letters came from the Middle West, Chicago, Cincinnati, Toledo, or from small towns in Michigan or Ohio. Once, a card all the way from San Francisco! Then, in October, Mama wrote that he was at home and that they would all come to Philadelphia for Thanksgiving. Thanksgiving! Perhaps they would stay for the concert on Saturday.

But Thanksgiving seemed very far away.

Mama wrote, "Papa is very busy engaging performers for the Pier for next season. He says to tell you that next Saturday is Papa Bucholz's birthday.

Please, Dailey, go to see him." Yes! thought Dai, it would be nice to see Mr. Bucholz again.

So, on Saturday, when Dai had finished his morning practice, he took Brin with him to visit Mr. Bucholz.

Brin found many things to investigate on the way and sometimes was so eager he pulled the lead from Dai's hand.

At last they reached the house. Dai rang the bell, and Mary, the maid, came to the door. Before Dai had time to stop him, Brin was inside, through the vestibule and into the hall. There, he stopped because Dai still held him fast, but he nearly upset Mary on his way.

"Excuse me, Mary," Dai said. "May I see Mr. Bucholz? It's his birthday, isn't it?"

"Yes, of course. How are you, Dailey? I will call Mr. Bucholz. Come in."

Brin, excited by the new surroundings, flew past Mary, scrambled around a great Chinese vase, setting it rocking, and clattered up the stairs. Dai, after him, still holding the leash. "Sorry, Mary," he said as he dashed past her. She was so startled she didn't have time to answer before Dai and Brin had vanished into the upstairs studio where Dai had first studied with Mr. Bucholz.

Through the open window, Dai heard a dog barking, but not before Brin had heard it! His ears stood up and with scarcely a pause he went into action. He leaped toward the window, jerking the leash from Dai's hand, and went *right on through,* screen and all—to the street! Dai rushed down the stairs, passing the astonished Mary, expecting to see Brin crushed to death.

Not so.

There was Brin, frisky as ever, a little startled by his fall, limping slightly but still in pursuit of the barking dog. He was nearly run over by a horse and wagon, and by the time he had crossed the street, the other dog had vanished.

He snuffled, looked puzzled, and trotted back to where Dai stood in astonishment at seeing Brin alive and well.

Mr. Bucholz met them at the foot of the stairs as Dai came in with Brin in his arms. Dai was still in a state of shock at Brin's leap into space, but finally remembered his manners and said, "Happy Birthday! Mr. Bucholz."

"Vell, vell," said Mr. Bucholz, bowing his thanks, "that's quite a dog you have there! Iss he always so impulsive?"

"Well, *some*times." Dai heaved a great sigh.

"Vell, he's gentle enough now, isn't he? How goes the music? Are you enjoying it at the Conservatory? I hope you are practicing, yes?"

Dai nodded, "Yes, it's great. But now we are getting ready for a concert after Thanksgiving. Mr. Schradiech wants me to be first chair but there are lots of rehearsals. It doesn't leave much time for baseball."

"Yes, I know, I know. But the fiddle will be your friend when you are too old for baseball—not? So, it pays to work at it, and you have a gift for it, don't forget. Not every boy has this gift for music; make the most of it, my boy."

Dai left Mr. Bucholz, determined to practice faithfully every day.

CHAPTER 12

It was late October. Lovely cool days took the place of summer's heat and haze and gave bright, sharp color to brick houses and trees lining the streets. It brought renewed energy, which often spilled out in boy fights at the school.

Kevin and Dai were always fighting and as quickly, making friends again. Dai sometimes had to defend his rights when teased, but he and Tim had become fast friends again after their fight. They walked home together every day. Walked? Ran, rather, hid behind trees, jumped out at each other from behind fences, wrestled over a coveted apple.

One Saturday morning the boys were playing ball on the corner lot. Dai was supposed to be practicing. He had pretty well mastered the exercise of sixty notes on one bow. But today it just wouldn't go. He tried again and fumbled it. And again. His fingers wouldn't respond. He sat down. It hurt to open and close his fist. Maybe I'm not cut out to be a fiddler, he thought. Out loud, but low, he said, "I'm sick of practicing. I'm *sick* of it! *Sick of it!*" He tossed his bow down and put the fiddle on the piano, then crossed to the door—yes, Aunt Em was still in the kitchen.

Brin was lying in the hall. Dai motioned for him
to follow and tiptoed through the vestibule, out of
the house, and ran down to join the boys in the
next block. Brin, crazy with joy, raced ahead of
him. As Tim reached for the ball, Brin jumped
for it, too, tripping him. Tim missed the ball and
kicked Brin out of the way. Dai, furious at seeing
Brin yelp with pain, leaped onto Tim, throwing
him to the pavement. As Tim went down with Dai
on top of him, Dai's left hand was caught between
Tim's shoulder and solid cement, sending a fiery
pain up his arm—his *left* hand, his *fiddle-string*
hand! Tim, pinned to the ground, pummeled Dai's
ribs and kicked to free himself. They rolled over and
over till finally, with a great heave, Tim pushed
Dai off and got to his feet. Dai held tight to his
left hand with his right, not knowing which hurt
the worst, hand or ribs. Tim shook himself, unhurt,
but angry, and said, "Take your crazy dog outa
my way!"

Dai turned and walked toward Aunt Em's with

Brin at his heels, followed by the jeering cries, "Yah! Yaa-ah! Tim's won again!"

Dai felt very sorry for himself.

Aunt Em met him at the door. "Where have you been?" she asked anxiously. "I suddenly realized that I hadn't heard your fiddle for the last few minutes. What's the matter?"

"Nothing. I just went out for a breath of air."

"Oh," Aunt Em said, but she kept on looking at Dai.

"Well, my hand hurts a little—"

"Your hand? Let me see. Ummm, it looks a little swollen. Come to the kitchen. We'll soak it again in hot water." She put the kettle on.

"Did you have another fight?"

Dai nodded. He didn't want to tell her about the fight. She didn't like fights any more than Mama did. Now, Aunt Em just looked at him, her mouth in a straight line. She poured hot water into a deep basin, then set a glass of milk before him and cut a crust from a loaf of freshly baked bread.

"Eat," she said. "Maybe you'll feel better. What's the matter with you anyway? Why are you so unhappy? Is it something I'm doing?"

Dai shook his head. His mouth was full.

"What then? Is it only that you must do your practicing?" Dai nodded. "Just think what it means to your father. He is paying a good deal for your musical education."

"I know, but I'm tired of always having to practice or go to rehearsal. None of the other boys have to."

"You'll be glad some day. Now, dry your hands and begin. It will all turn out for the best. You'll see."

Dai nodded, halfheartedly and went back to his practicing.

The hot water hadn't helped much. The fingers of his left hand seemed all thumbs on the fiddle strings. Even the bow seemed more difficult to handle. He sat down, discouraged. Maybe I'm just not good for anything, he thought. I lost the fight and I can't play the fiddle very well. I think I won't try to play at the concert. I guess I'll just go back to Atlantic City where I belong, he thought. Aunt Em's good to me, but she isn't my mother and this isn't my home. He got up to put away the fiddle, but as he covered it with the velvet pad, he wondered how Mama would feel if he walked in and surprised her. She might faint. He remembered how he had said to Papa—*I promise.* He stood for a moment more—thinking—then quickly took up the fiddle again, picked up the bow, and, counting under his breath, played the sixty notes on one bow. It hurt a good deal but Dai went on with his practice. By the time the hour was up, his hand was hurting badly again; still he had kept his promise, and in a few days his hand was better though still somewhat stiff.

When he went for his lesson on Saturday, Peter Androssi was still in the studio finishing his lesson.

Arky came in with his violin case and music. He too heard Peter.

"That guy can really play!" he said.

"Yeah. What's he got that I haven't got?"

"He hasn't anything you don't have if you'd only *practice*," Arky declared. "I've heard you bring tone out of that fiddle of yours that makes the chills run down your back!"

"Do you think Peter practices all that much?"

"Well, maybe not. But I think he just loves it so much that he plays all the time. I wish *I* could play as he does. I practice and practice but it doesn't come out like Peter's!" Arky said ruefully. "See you at rehearsal."

Peter's lesson was over. He came out, grinned at the boys, and went into another part of the school. "See ya!" he said.

Mr. Schradiech called Dai in for his lesson. He noticed that Dai's hand was rather unsteady with the bow and his fingering unsure.

"What's the matter with your hand now?"

Dai had to tell him about the second fight.

"Boys *will* fight occasionally, I know, but for violinists it is not good. Suppose you repeat that passage."

After the lesson, boys and girls from classes in the Conservatory assembled for the rehearsal, Arky and Peter among them.

The exciting, atonal sound of instruments tuning up began. Henry's horn blared out, Dorothea struck the A on the piano, the fiddles buzzed and droned. Then, Mr Schradiech rapped for attention and the rehearsal went on. They played through the whole program except for the solos, with many stops for correction and guidance.

Walking home after the rehearsal, Dai began to feel lonesome again. Tim and the other boys in his class at school weren't interested in the symphony orchestra. It seemed to him he never had time to do anything but lessons, practice, and rehearsals. And no one to talk to except Aunt Em and Brin.

He hadn't even had time to build a house for Brin. But Aunt Em had said he could sleep in the shed when the weather turned cold. He guessed she was a pretty good sort after all.

That afternoon when he got home she asked Dai to go on an errand. "You can take Brin if you want to and go to Kolb's Bakery. I've suddenly run out of bread. Sometimes I forget how much a boy eats!"

Dai and Brin started off happily.

All was quiet till they passed a row of houses set very high above a flight of steps where a man was painting the porch. Just then, a cat came into view and started up the steps. Brin leaped forward so suddenly, the leash slipped from Dai's hand. Up Brin flew after the cat, over the porch, slippery with paint, and on down the steps, splashing paint as he came, landing at Dai's feet dripping with paint.

"KEEP THAT ANIMAL WHERE HE BE-LONGS!" the man yelled, shaking his fist at Dai, who stood speechless. He pulled a few blades of grass to try and clean the paint off Brin's legs and feet.

"Here," yelled the man, "use this!" He threw down the paint rag he carried.

Dai rubbed and scrubbed at Brin's legs and hindquarters till most of the paint had been wiped off, then returned the rag to the man saying, "Thanks, I'm sorry."

"You *better* be, and you better keep that animal under control."

Brin sat meekly at the foot of the steps and quietly followed Dai down the street.

What would Aunt Em say? Would she let him keep Brin? He worried all the way home.

Aunt Em met him at the door.

"Whatever happened?" she said, as Brin came rushing in showing his green back and legs. When Dai told her the story, instead of being angry, she began to chuckle, then to laugh, then to cry with laughter. She sat down and wiped her eyes with her apron. "Oh, oh—" she gasped. "It's *so funny.*"

At last, she recovered her dignity and her breath.

"Well," she said, "let's clean him up and feed him. I expect he's hungry."

Dai sighed with relief. He was glad Aunt Em had the de Angeli sense of humor. Somehow life seemed a little more normal.

As time for the concert drew near, Mr. Schradiech called for frequent rehearsals. He included in his teaching suggestions for concert stage behavior, walking in a dignified way, standing erect while playing solo, and bowing gracefully when applauded. Dai and Arky decided there was more to playing in a symphony orchestra than they had realized. But it was exciting!

At each rehearsal Dai could sense that the students' playing was more sure and the sound of the various instruments more unified. Dai's hand improved every day. At home he went over and over the violin parts of the concerto he was to perform. Sometimes Aunt Em filled in the other parts on the piano. That was a big help and Dai was sure he was showing improvement. At rehearsal one afternoon in November, Mr. Schradiech commended the boys and girls for their faithful practice, but he called Dai aside for a special talk.

"I'm afraid that hand of yours is interfering with the smooth performance you were beginning to achieve. Perhaps we'd better put Peter in first chair." He turned to Peter. "And, Peter, don't forget your music next time. Three at one stand is too much. I'm sorry, Dailey, but violinists shouldn't be fist fighters."

Dai's heart sank. He had written Mama he was to be concertmeister.

Well, there it was. He couldn't be.

"Cheer up!" Mr. Schradiech comforted him. "Perhaps next time!"

The week of Thanksgiving arrived. The last rehearsal for the concert was to be given in Musical Fund Hall.

All forty of the students from various classes in the Conservatory made up the orchestra. Peter, Dai, and Arky, with several others played violin with Peter in first chair now. Juliet Carter led the violas. Dorothea Carrol, piano, Sam Dager and two other boys, cello. There were two bass fiddles and Henry Kuhn played French horn. It was a thrilling sound when they all played together.

As they were about to begin the first selection at

that last rehearsal, Peter discovered he had left his bow at home.

"So—" Mr. Schradiech said, looking quite severe. "How will you play without your fiddle bow, eh?" Mr. Schradiech looked annoyed. Peter looked red and embarrassed.

"Well, I suppose I can lend you my bow, for this time only. I hope you will learn to put everything in its place or you will never amount to anything!"

Mr. Schradiech took his bow from the case and gave it to Peter.

The rehearsal went on.

Dai played his solo part perfectly. His hand was almost healed. He wished Mr. Schradiech would reinstate him in first chair. But Peter, too, played his solo perfectly and there was hardly a mistake in the symphony. Once or twice, Mr. Schradiech rapped his baton for attention when Isabel knocked the music off the stand and when Arky fumbled a turn. But at the end of the rehearsal, he praised the work they had done.

"Don't forget!" he said, emphasizing it with the baton, "sometimes a good final rehearsal makes us *too* confident. Know that you must still practice, still reach for perfect performance. Be sure to remember your fiddles and bows—" he looked especially to Peter—"look your best—and good-by till Saturday." He waved them all out of the hall.

Aunt Em took Dai to Strawbridge and Clothier and bought him a new suit, a white shirt, and black silk tie. His arms had grown too long for his other best suit.

Then followed a busy time at Aunt Em's. There was much bustling about getting beds made up, cleaning and dusting. There was no school the day before Thanksgiving. Dai scrubbed the white marble steps for her, carried extra boards for the dining table, and went with her to market.

"You can carry the turkey and all the extras needed for the Thanksgiving dinner," she said, "and the food we need for the rest of the week, while the family's here." They took two big market baskets with them to Ninth Street.

How good it would be to see the family again! Dai could hardly wait till afternoon, but marketing took up most of the morning.

Aunt Em had made pepper pot for supper with fresh fruit for dessert. The apple pie was for tomorrow. It stood on the shelf with the freshly baked bread, giving off heavenly odors. The ice box was filled with cranberry sauce, applesauce, and other good things.

At last, they were there.

"Where's my boy?" Mama called when Aunt Em opened the door. Dai was there in seconds. How good it was to see Mama's brown eyes twinkling, to hear her laugh, to feel Grandma's hug and Papa's arms around him.

"We heard you playing as we came along the street," Papa said. "It sounded very professional. How is it going?"

"Great!—but I'm not to play first chair as I told you. You see, I hurt my hand. It's better now, but—" Dai's voice trailed off.

Papa nodded. "Hummmm," he murmured, "I see. Fighting, eh?" Dai nodded, too.

"Well, you'll learn—I hope."

After everyone was settled in rooms, things unpacked, they gathered in the dining room to be near Aunt Em, who was in and out of the kitchen, setting the table and getting the food ready for supper.

There was the usual talk of everyone's health and how Mama had improved in the seashore air, the weather, and how Dai was getting on in the Brothers' school and at the Conservatory. Then Papa had stories to tell about his western tour, how each city had its special quality and style, quite different from Philadelphia. "I think of all the cities I've been in, San Francisco is most beautiful. Still, it hasn't the charm of history that Philadelphia has, and of course, the best city in the world is where the family is." Everyone agreed.

Thanksgiving Day and the two days following seemed to fly and it was almost time for the concert. Music filled the evenings and Dailey surprised Papa with the improvement in his playing. Mama and Grandma Craig smiled proudly and Aunt Em said, "There's our boy! Doesn't he do well?"

Papa said, "Grandfather Benedict would be proud of the sound you bring out of his fiddle strings! *I'm* proud of you. Too bad you had to fight and hurt your hand so you can't be first chair. But— better luck next time." He put his arm around Dai's shoulder.

As Dai thought about playing in the big hall, his

stomach felt queer. He played his solo over and over while the others listened. Aunt Em tried to coax him to eat at supper, but for once, he wasn't hungry.

Papa understood. "I know how it is. I still have butterflies when it's time for an opening of the show. It puts one on his mettle! Keyed up to do his best. You will, I'm sure."

Dai wasn't so sure.

Mama fussed over him as he dressed for the concert as she had always done.

He wished she wouldn't. Still, he thought, it is rather nice to be fussed over again.

It was time to go to the hall. Many of the boys and girls had arrived when Dai came. Arky was there and Dai could see Peter tuning his fiddle. He wondered if they felt as nervous as he did. Certainly they didn't show it.

Soon, the performers were tuning and testing their instruments and the thrill of hearing it was indescribable.

Promptly at eight o'clock, Mr. Schradiech sent them out onto the platform to find their places. Dai wished he had been concertmeister, but as Mr. Schradiech said, "You may be thankful that you can play at all after injuring your hand."

There were flowers at the edge of the platform, the chairs arranged so that two could share a music stand, and Dai sat next to Peter.

When all were settled in place, Mr. Schradiech came in and stood at the podium.

The first number on the program was a Mozart piano concerto, and as soon as the music started, the peculiar feeling in Dai's stomach left him. He was a part of an orchestra, a part of the interweaving harmony. Henry Kuhn played the slow movement from a Mozart composition for French horn in perfect pianissimo.

There followed a solo by Arky, one of Fritz Kreisler's compositions, then a Handel-Auer Sonata, played by Peter Androssi, Dorothea's piano solo, then, as the last number, a Mendelssohn violin concerto—the violin part played by Dailey de Angeli.

When Dai stood up to play with the orchestra accompaniment, he was determined to bring out all the violin had to offer, to play with feeling, to show Papa he was keeping his promise.

He came in promptly at the appointed place, remembered all the turns and pauses, ending with a flourish. He felt happy.

Parents and friends gathered around the young musicians who all wore the smile of satisfaction in work well done. Mr. Schradiech complimented them on their performance and shook the hand of each one saying, "You conducted yourselves like professionals. I'm proud of you!"

"Yes," Dai thought, "that is just what I will be. A professional!"

About the Author

MARGUERITE DE ANGELI was born on March 14, 1889, in Lapeer, Michigan. Since her first children's story appeared in 1935, she has written twenty-three books for young readers which have won her a large and faithful audience and many top awards as well. In 1946, *Bright April* was named an Honor Book by the New York *Herald Tribune*. In 1950, *The Door in the Wall* earned the Newbery Medal, and in 1961 it won a Lewis Carroll Shelf Award. In 1968, Mrs. de Angeli was awarded the Regina Medal by the Catholic Library Association for excellence in writing for young people. A mother of five, grandmother of thirteen, and great-grandmother of three, Mrs. de Angeli has found her own family to be a vital source of her special insight into the imagination of children; each of her books reflects the wisdom and personal warmth that have earned her a special place in the hearts of generations of young readers.

DATE DUE